moo of writing

Other books by Nan Lundeen

POETRY

The Pantyhose Declarations

Black Dirt Days: Poems as Memoir

moo of writing

how to milk your potential

nan lundeen

Cow art by Cynthia Morgan, camorganwrites.com

Cover design and publishing services by John Adam Wickliffe, wickliffe.net

Grateful acknowledgment is made to Sally Lou Maxey for use of her poem that begins, "Poised in paradox."

Printed in the United States of America.

In memory of Sylvia Barclay, my mentor, who said, "Pass it on."

My thanks to my husband Ron DeKett for editing reincarnations of Moo of Writing until the cows came home, to Cynthia Morgan whose whimsical drawings moo on the page, and to John Adam Wickliffe on whose design and digital magic I rely.

— Nan Lundeen

Poised in paradox, my heart is empty, yet full . . .
Yearning and fulfilled.

— Sally Lou Maxey

contents

with every chapter:
• meditation
• writing exercises
• tips

moo of writing

how to milk your potential

nan lundeen

introduction

Consider the cow. She stands in the meadow swishing her tail and chewing her cud, at peace with the trees, with the breeze, and with her companions. A dairy cow can produce five gallons of milk every day.

Like the cow, the writer ruminates, taking in the fodder of life, digesting it in the subconscious, and turning it into creative material waiting for release. When the writer relaxes, words flow. Moo of Writing will help you milk your writing potential.

The process is exercise, relaxation, including freewriting, and meditation.

Scientists are discovering new ways that exercise and meditation benefit the mind. Cutting-edge research using new technology confirms connections between relaxation and creativity. Free your creativity and delight in the flow of stories you'll find hidden inside.

Moo workshop writer Angie Feltman describes what she discovered: "My book of stories is right there in my mind."

Ah, at last—a method whereby creative writing springs from our pens like crocuses popping through snow!

Not quite, although sometimes it seems as if stories write themselves. Behind the effortlessness lies a commitment to daily writing, yet it needn't gobble time. You could choose to walk around your neighborhood or do yoga for ten minutes, spend five minutes in meditation, and devote ten minutes to freewriting. Or, you could make a longer time commitment. Whether you devote minimum or maximum time, a routine will establish a habit of writing freely that will jump-start your creativity. You won't find relief from research or grueling edits and rewrites, but when you practice Moo of Writing, you will coax your stories and poems onto the page.

This handbook will provide you with the tools to implement this exciting process. Each chapter builds on the previous chapter, helping you learn the process step-by-step. At the end of each chapter, you'll find a meditation, writing exercises, and writing tips. Approach the method holistically. It works best when you practice all three: exercise, relaxation, and meditation. Think of them as equal sides of a triangle.

Shall we begin?

chapter 1
get your moodle on

Cows are Zen masters, writers benefit when they behave like them, and science concurs.

Observe cows closely and you will notice their ears flicker from time to time when they're listening to the beat of *moo*, a sound that also is spelled *mu*. Mu is a centuries-old Zen koan, a phrase or question that leads to contemplation. Unfathomable and resistant to definition, mu tosses rational thought out the barn door and invites a different perspective.

Relax when you write and simultaneously work hard. Mu invites you to step aside and get out of your own way. When you stay out of your way, you find your way. No matter how you spell it, Moo is a feeling of being relaxed and focused almost as if someone else were writing the words or pitching the ball or playing the music. It's a smooth energy that delights the soul. Here's the hitch—it's so productive, writers have a hard time believing in it.

Good ideas meander in when they feel welcome. To welcome them, begin with exercise. Exercise helps free the mind from anger, obsessions, anxiety, and petty details. It releases endorphins that ease depression. Stress hounds many of us daily and hampers sound sleep. Physically removing negative emotions from the mind-body benefits writing. Swimming, gardening, bicycling, taking a daily walk, working out at the gym, practicing yoga or tai chi, or any type of exercise you enjoy sets you on your own Moo path. If you're already exercising, congratulations! If not, think about the benefits and make up your mind to give it a try.

Moo workshop writer Adamy Damaris Diaz decided to work toward a Moo attitude and "zens" out while she runs with her husband. "The changes in my life start with the changes in my mind," she says.

State-of-the-art science is confirming what wise writers have known all along—exercise, relaxation, and meditation tap into a sweet spot from which creativity flows.

Studies by researchers at Stanford University show that walking boosts creative inspiration; one measurement of creativity increased eighty-one percent. Overall, creative output increased an average of sixty percent when walking compared with sitting, according to *Stanford Report*, April 24, 2014. Walking outside worked best, but tramping on a treadmill worked, too. Furthermore, their research showed that the creativity boost lasted for a time after participants sat down. It's important to note, however, that while some cognitive functions relating to creative inspiration increased, focus did not. We'll address how to improve focus in chapter 6.

Here's encouraging news out of that study—walkers benefited from as little as ten minutes of walking daily!

Brenda Ueland, whose book, *If You Want to Write*, has motivated writers for decades, and who could inspire a toad to write, walked five miles every day. Her richest ideas appeared toward the end of relaxing walks when she practiced being aware in the present and did not try to think. Trying to think doesn't work, and neither does trying *not* to think.

Mu.

Ueland even bundled up for walks around Lake Harriet in Minneapolis when the mercury sank to minus eighteen degrees Fahrenheit. Without her walks, she felt like Mrs. Gummidge in *David Copperfield*, a miserable character who sits inside beside the fire and feels grumpy.

If you are disabled or physically challenged, consider consulting your physician on an exercise program that would suit your needs. If you can't exercise, you will still benefit from the tools this handbook provides to assist your writing.

As it is with much of life, balance is required. A productive Moo writer balances exercise that nourishes body and mind, and quietude that feeds the soul.

Gain quietude through relaxation and meditation. A handy relaxation tool Ueland recommends is "moodling." Moodlers putter, daydream, and listen to the flutter of fairy wings. They reject a mindset that sits them down determined to hurry up and produce. If you try to hurry ideas along, they scurry under the nearest rock, and only the faintest glimmer of an eyeball or two peeks out from the dark. Ideas are shy creatures who want to be coaxed out to play.

Researchers in psychology and brain science at the University of California, Santa Barbara, find that mind-wandering facilitates creative incubation. Jonathan Schooler, Ph.D., a leading researcher in the field, found that creative thinking improves when people begin a task, take a break that involves non-demanding behavior, and then return to the first task.

For instance, let's say you're writing happily away when your mind clouds, and you're muddled about what to write next. How about moodling to clear up your muddle? You might strum your guitar, play a hand of solitaire, or water your plants. Any of these would be more productive than motoring on and smashing into a brick wall.

How dare we moodle when the world demands that we conform to its frenetic pace?

Unless we are hermits, if we move more slowly than the world expects, the hurry-up bully inside us cracks his whip.

How do we tame him?

Even retirees who finally have time to themselves find sloughing him off challenging. We must produce every waking moment! That mindset is what Vietnamese-born Thich Nhat Hanh, a Buddhist monk, calls "habit energy."

Do we really need to hurry about doing, doing, doing, or is this particular bully actually a big fat habit?

Negative habits are tough buggers to overcome, but positive habits help you relax and harness your creativity.

Moodling is an important Moo writing tool. I like to use a broad definition of "moodling" to include rumination. Similar to daydreaming, rumination is the stuff that goes on in the back of your head when you're thinking about something else. It's also the gentle wanderings you travel when falling asleep—unless, of course, you're in that monkey mind mode that scurries about unproductively and keeps you awake. Nudge your mind toward whatever creative project you'd like to moodle on, letting it float above your bed like a balloon. You'll wake up the next morning (or the middle of the night) with ideas.

It helps enormously to dedicate a spot in your house to rumination. To slow down, we need a meadow of our own like our friends, the cows, even if it's a small space. We may not be able to luxuriate in an entire meadow, but we can make do with a corner of our own.

You could, of course, get away from it all at the beach, a cabin in the mountains, a retreat center of any sort, including one that caters to writers, or travel to any idyllic spot around the globe. I urge you, however, to establish a corner of your own for daily practice. Don't wait for that special time. Make every day special.

If you find it impossible to set aside a spot, such as a window seat, a floor cushion in the corner of a book-lined den, or a deep, comfy chair on a porch or deck, consider claiming space outside your home. Would a park, a library, or a blanket under a tree work for you? If your life requires a schedule, carve out do-nothing time. If you worry that you'll lose yourself in your ruminations and never return, set an alarm so you needn't heed a clock until reminded of your responsibilities.

A meadow of your own nurtures creativity. Deprived of an oasis, your creative self risks shriveling from neglect. I call my oasis my ruminating rocker. It's a cherry, Shaker-style rocker with a woven seat and back in burgundy and blue that sits beside a window overlooking our bird feeders and two fir trees.

Experience Moo in any form or combination that works for you. If you're into multi-tasking, combine exercise, relaxation, and meditation. Do freewriting as soon as you can after your session.

I do recommend meditation as a separate daily practice, although you can exercise mindfully and derive similar benefits.

Pulitzer Prize winning author Alice Walker, who wrote *The Color Purple* and many other wonderful books, describes meditation as a "loyal friend" that helped her write her books.

Contemporary Western science is building a body of evidence on the benefits of meditation in an emerging field called contemplative neuroscience. It uses the Western empirical approach to study the effects of meditation on areas such as focus, compassion, stress reduction, and physical and mental health. A leading researcher in contemplative practices, Richard J. Davidson, Ph.D., a neuroscientist at the University of Wisconsin, is one of several who brings the Dalai Lama and other spiritual leaders of the contemplative tradition together with the world's top scientists in mind-body medicine for dialogue.

For our purposes, it is enough to know that current science supports the premise that relaxation sparks creativity. The concept isn't new, but the technology for researching it is. Stories of inventors and scientists to whom break-through ideas came while they were in a relaxed state are commonplace.

The story of Thomas Edison is one of my favorites because it elicits a memorable image.

Edison systematically mined the ideas that came to him in a relaxed state, according to Daniel Goleman, Paul Kaufman, and Michael Ray, who wrote *The Creative Spirit*. The authors report that Edison would sit in a chair, his hands extending over the chair arms, each hand holding a ball bearing. Two pie plates would sit on the floor beneath them. When Edison relaxed, his hands opened, and the bearings clanked onto the plates, alerting him. He would immediately write down what had been running through his mind.

Psychologist Joydeep Bhattacharya, Ph.D., a leading researcher in neuroscience, psychology, and creativity at the University of London, finds connections between relaxation and that aha! moment, suggesting that relaxation makes the mind more susceptible to creative ideas.

Scientific studies on the subject result in headlines such as: "Relax the brain for that Eureka! moment," *www.telegraph.co.uk.*, (1-23-08), "Want To Be Creative? Let Your Mind Wander," *www.psychologytoday.com/blog/choke*, (10-10-12), "Why great ideas come when you aren't trying," *www.nature.com*, (5-21-12), "Discovering the Virtues of a Wandering Mind," *The New York Times*, (6-28-10), and "No lotus position needed: Neuroscience pushes meditation into the mainstream," *Minneapolis Star Tribune*, (5-29-13).

It's as if researchers were discovering the why and how of wisdom that talented writers such as Ray Bradbury shared with readers decades ago. Bradbury published *Zen in the Art of Writing*, a collection of essays on creativity in which he holds that the wise writer knows his own subconscious.

A busy mind can't tap into the well of abundance that lies in the subconscious. It's relaxation that leads to insight.

None of this happens without deep breathing.

How we breathe affects our mental and physical states. When we are scared or worried or in a horrendous hurry, we take shallow, quick breaths. Sometimes, we hold our breath. If we slow our breathing, panic subsides. We gain control.

Deep breathing is a simple tool necessary to Moo of Writing. The muse blesses best our slow, alpha brain waves. Several Moo techniques incorporate deep breathing, such as centering ourselves with a Moo stone or listening to our gut or recognizing the true face of our fears. We'll discuss them and practice the techniques in chapters to come.

We writers live inside our heads, but we're also curious. We really look at things, study people, wonder at the stars. We peer at the moon through binoculars as if we were still kids. We observe and ruminate, chewing our cud. Moo practice will help us keenly observe what passes in front of our life screens.

When you breathe deeply and observe what is around you, you soon begin wondering, and the creative process begins. It is a gentle process. The habit of awareness that you cultivate will pay off when you write description. For instance, if a scene takes place in a gourmet grocery, visit one and observe. Inhale, watch, take notes. Hang out with herbed olives, shiny green peppers, baby French green beans, and Tanzanian coffee.

It's possible to relax, breathe, and observe at the same time. The process draws you out of your busy mind and carries you to a more peaceful place. Wrap your arms around silence. Sit and listen to your heart. However it happens, relaxation is a key to tapping into the flow.

Moo with the muse. Ideas and phrases putter about the universe on their own, oblivious to writers' needs. It's ineffective to call them while standing in a corncrib door hollering, "Soooooooooeee!" as if they were hogs. They're free spirits. If you set out the iced tea beside a rocking chair, they'll come sit a spell.

counting meditation

Listen to Nan lead this meditation at nanlundeen.com.

An easy way to rest your mind and prepare yourself for Moo of Writing is to meditate on your breaths. In this meditation, we count to four as we inhale, and again count to four as we exhale. Then we repeat. I have chosen the number four to represent the four elements—air, fire, water, earth.

Lie down or sit with your spine straight and your feet flat on the floor. Focus on your breath. Breathe slowly and deeply. Count silently. Breathe in: one—two—three—four. Breathe out: one—two—three—four. Breathe in: one—two—three—four. Breathe out: one—two—three—four. Continue breathing and counting. When thoughts intrude, let them drift by like fluffy clouds on a warm summer day. Continue breathing and counting as long as you like. When you are ready, come back to the here and now.

writing exercises

- Sit outdoors or gaze through a window for at least five minutes. Write what you observe. Keen observation enriches the imagination. For example, on a walk on the outskirts of DeWitt, Iowa, where I was visiting my mother, I was blown away by the images that fell upon my eye. They gave me a poem.

> In the Distance, a Farm Yard
>
> > Take a walk with me
> > down the last sidewalk
> > at the edge of town.
> >
> > At dusk
> > red sky bleeds
> > into black earth.
> >
> > Look, over there
> > a lone pole light
> > casts a yellow cone
> > across a fallow field.
> >
> > This is Iowa.

- Choose a piece of writing that you particularly admire. It may be fiction, nonfiction, or poetry. Decide upon one word that describes the piece, revealing what you most admire about the work. Then, reflect upon how your own writing exhibits that attribute. Here are examples Moo workshop writers chose: *The Pearl* by John Steinbeck—humanity. *Their Eyes Were Watching God* by Zora Neale Hurston—emotion. *Anam Cara* by John O'Donohue—depth. Is expression of the attribute you admire a goal you would like to set for your work? Eventually, you will want to choose several goals, but for now, concentrate on the most important.

tips

- Clarity is the mama cow of all tips. Above all, be clear. If you're tempted to break a grammar rule, go ahead, but not at the expense of clarity. For instance, we've been taught to write in complete sentences.

Does that mean *always?*

No. In a personal essay, I wrote:

> I like different a lot, and you were different, and so was your buddy who lived with you at a place you called Clearhouse. Irony in a name. Thick with it. You could have scraped it off the back porch with a shovel, but I didn't see it.

I chose to use phrases in that paragraph for rhythm and emphasis. It's punchier than something wordier and grammatically correct such as, "There was a lot of irony in that name. In fact, it was thick with it."

- Sharpen an image until it bristles. I have an actual, "bristly" example to share with you. I wrote a poem, "Blackberry Stars," about one of my earliest memories of my father. He appeared at the edge of our woods with a bucketful of blackberries in each hand and smiling broadly. I wrote "grinning," which was apt. But I never could quite capture the image until I remembered asking my mother what was stuck to Daddy's overalls. I was worried they would hurt him, and was assured they wouldn't. I had sharpened the image until it bristled when I wrote the words, "overalls stickered with cockleburs." Here's an excerpt:

> My child's eye
> filled with Daddy
> when you appeared
> at woods' edge
>
> grinning
>
> overalls stickered with cockleburs

- Do you read? A whole bunch? Good! It'll jump-start your writing whether you write poetry or prose. It's vital to be aware of what's being published in your own genre, and it's mind-expanding to dip your hoof into other genres. If you write, read. If by some strange circumstance you're stuck and can't write, read more. (If you practice Moo, getting stuck is unlikely.)

moo notes

moo notes

chapter 2
moo with the habit loop

Cows must be milked every day. Twice a day, actually. On the Iowa farm where I grew up, our dairy cows followed a path home morning and evening to be milked. Living near them created a lovely rhythm. Similarly, daily freewriting will facilitate the flow of words. An open pathway between mind and pen creates magic.

When you feel relaxed after exercise or meditation, write without restriction the first words that come into your mind. What you hear in your head goes directly onto the page. Don't skip the exercise or meditation.

One Moo workshop writer said that "crap" poured onto her freewriting pages for months before she wrote anything creative. What do you think was going on? Yep, she hadn't been meditating or exercising, no swishing of the tail in a quiet meadow first. No alpha waves. Her busy beta waves had commandeered her pen.

It's best, however, to avoid judging your words. The *process* of freewriting is vastly more important than *what* you write. Moo workshop writer Cindy Hosea likens freewriting to stretching before exercise.

You may not realize what you're thinking until the words roll onto the page. The relationship between the brain and the pen turns up surprises. Using language is a complex task that calls upon all that you know and all that lies hidden within you. You'll make startling, magical discoveries and fall in love with writing all over again.

Is freewriting the same as writing in a journal?

No.

Journal writing usually involves observation, sifting memories, or processing ideas or experiences such as commenting on something. Writers value the process because it synthesizes and reveals. It complements freewriting, but doesn't replace it.

Freewriting is spontaneous. Boom! Onto the page. Mind and pen merge. Remember, what you're free to write you're free to destroy so don't fear hurting someone. No censoring allowed.

How would you establish a habit of daily freewriting? Through good intentions? Willpower? Discipline? Those might work, but many writers clasp frustration to their chests and wander through the pastures of their lives moaning pitifully that they can't get any writing done.

Could science help?

Researchers at the Massachusetts Institute of Technology found that our brains form habit loops consisting of three steps: cue, routine, reward. A cue is something that ignites a routine behavior without thought, such as your email dings. A routine is the habitual behavior you follow after the cue—you open the email. The reward is what you get out of the behavior.

I find the cue to be a powerful impetus. For instance, I do yoga while following instructions on a video. When I turn the video on, the familiar music acts as my cue. Automatically, I unroll my yoga mat and take off my socks.

Your daily writing cue could be pouring your second cup of coffee in the morning or tucking the kids into bed at night; your routine could be ten minutes of uninhibited writing; your reward, whatever appears on the page.

Envision a loop that would work for you.

If you've already established a daily writing routine, adjust your loop to add freewriting. Eliminate cues that trigger interruptive behavior. For instance, turn off your email dinger.

But how do we turn off that master inhibitor, the inner critic?

I call mine Cecil. Cecil lures me into automatically censoring myself before my fingers translate from my brain. He commandeers the aid of yammering lies such as *you're not good enough or this is a waste of time or you'll embarrass yourself.*

Drag his scheming cohorts out into the light. They'll blink up at you helplessly, and you'll recognize them for what they are: cowardly twits that thrive on darkness and inertia. They're ecstatic when your brain runs in grooves; they abhor leaps of imagination. Cecil feels safest when you methodically follow a narrow track like a cable car inching with mechanical dependency up a precipitous mountainside. The mountainside may in reality be only a bump in the road.

As inhibiting as Cecil can be, you've created him for a reason. Most likely he's trying to protect you based on past experience. Maybe he squirreled away a memory of you being mocked as a child for a spontaneous act, and he's trying to shield you from ridicule and shame. His reasons to shy away from risks may be legion, and you may never unearth them all.

The Moo way would be to reassure him, not battle him. Battle will make him stronger. Be assured, if you acknowledge his concerns and promise him that you will take care of yourself, he will ease up. He'll sit in a corner observing you but not interfering like a cat that you hope loves you but seldom purrs.

How do we persuade him to reveal his concerns?

Some Moo writers find it helpful to fill two pages quickly with inner critic negativities, listing reasons why they can't write their truth. As the negativities pour out, a truly revealing one will pop out—it will be an aha! moment.

Once you've revealed the messages skulking under the surface of your mind, be aware that fear feeds Cecil and leads us to distrust ourselves. If we let ourselves run free . . . ah, the horror. Self-distrust may be the initial creepy-crawly the writer drags into the light. Take a good look at the weak, wicked thing. Its treacherous heart pounds with lies: *you are good only if you keep strict control of yourself; other people will not like you if you reveal your true self; you think you have talent? Ha!*

When you've identified Cecil's chatter, set it aside and listen to your true, creative voice. He may mean well, but don't let Cecil's messages paralyze you. Plumb them for wisdom and detach from them, keeping what's useful and addressing the issues.

A caveat—the inner critic has astonishing staying power because he's all about helping you survive, albeit, he's misguided. If necessary, reassure him repeatedly.

Some Moo writers say they hear no internal negative comments. Are they productive writers? If yes, all is well. If not, and if they truly want to write (an important *if*), Cecil is triumphing from his burrow. Those writers will benefit most of all from listing why they aren't writing. They're usually buying into their own lies such as, "I just can't find the time" or "I'm going to start writing as soon as . . .." When the list, written quickly and spontaneously, grows longer, the truth will out.

Will the list empower Cecil?

No. You need to know what truths lie beneath his well-intentioned lies. Wield awareness as a tool to build a positive frame of mind. Observe your list coolly as if you were a mathematician surveying a list of equations. Are any of them valid? Valid or invalid, gently reassure Cecil. Address his concerns.

How?

Let's say your list reveals a prediction that if you write unfettered, you'll be labeled a show-off. When you think about that, you remember that you were labeled a show-off by jealous high school competitors when you let your talents shine.

Create an affirmation to address Cecil's concern. An affirmation is a positive statement specific to a problem written in present tense. You are affirming that the positive outcome is already happening; repeat it often. Display the affirmation around your work space; make it part of your desktop; write it in your journal often.

Written repetition is powerful, especially before you begin your daily freewriting. It's a good way to encourage yourself, building strength and self-confidence. An affirmation to address the above example is, *my true friends appreciate my talent.*

Eventually, as you write freely, you'll hear a line that sounds like a first line of a story, a poem, an essay, or a novel. Maybe you'll hear a title. You'll hear yourself saying, *I wonder . . .* You'll realize, *that's a short story or, it would be fun to write about X.* Freewriting entices imaginative first drafts onto the page.

Follow your fingers.

A Moo writer asked, "How do I know when my freewriting is done?"

The answer is—it's never done.

The writing is just there. Simply step into the flow and out again. Follow the cows home to be milked and back out to pasture again.

Most of us admire self-control, but to tap the flow, let go. Are you afraid that if you let go, you'll expose something you don't like about yourself? You *will* expose something—the sad, sweet, morose, scary, funny, fanciful, inspiring, courageous, powerful, cynical, nostalgic stories we all carry within us. They're wonderful; they reflect life.

To access them, establish a habit loop. Daily practice is vital to the flow.

flowing words meditation

Listen to Nan lead this meditation at nanlundeen.com.

Lie down or sit with your spine straight and your feet
flat on the floor. Focus on your breath. Place one palm
up open to good energies and one palm down to ground
yourself. Breathe slowly and deeply. Silently count your
breaths. Breathe in: one—two—three—four. Breathe out:
one—two—three—four. Breathe in: one—two—three—
four. Breathe out: one—two—three—four. Continue
breathing and counting. When thoughts intrude, let
them drift by like fluffy clouds on a warm summer day.
Continue deep breathing and counting. When you feel
relaxed, imagine yourself walking to a small, calm body of
water such as a pond, an inlet, or a lagoon. Sit beside it or
walk into it and sit down, whichever is more comfortable
for you. Breathe. Relax. All is well. Imagine your scene
of beauty in detail. Do you see rocks? Do you hear gulls?
Do you see a white egret? The water is warm, and you are
safe. Rest your hand on the gently rippling water. Breathe.
When you are ready, open your eyes and know that a flow
of words is yours.

writing exercise

- Make an appointment with yourself for daily physical exercise of your choice and freewriting. Set a realistic minimum time. Experiment with cue-routine-reward. Begin today.

tips

- Stick with your daily relaxation and freewriting routine no matter whether creating, editing, rewriting, or polishing works in progress. For some, the practice best facilitates the flow first thing in the morning. For others, nighttime works best. You might try relaxation and freewriting twice daily, morning and evening. Discover what works for you.

- Meditative music invites alpha waves.

- Writing projects can capriciously emit an energy of their own. When a piece of work is flowing, stay with it. Don't abandon it lest it become a calf bawling piteously in the pasture.

- Freewriting can be used to open up a work in progress. Wherever you're at with the work, let words flow whether they make sense or not until something clicks.

When do we open the spigot?

a) When you're writing a first draft.

b) When a work in progress is flat and you want to perk it up.

c) When you need to add a transition. (Expand your work just enough to make the connection.)

d) When you need to add examples or expound to clarify a work in progress.

e) For fun.

moo notes

moo notes

chapter 3
the moo of me

Memorable writing engages emotion.

Do you want to clobber your readers with feeling or brush them gently with a wisp? Either way, when emotion is handled well, writing sticks with readers.

Why does Tiny Tim, the cheerful, ailing child from Charles Dickens's *A Christmas Carol,* live on for centuries?

Dickens packs an emotional wallop into this short book.

His life's work is anchored in his own childhood during which his father was put in debtor's prison, and he was forced for a time to live alone and work at an odious job. Dickens specializes in characters who depict the vulnerable child such as Tiny Tim, Oliver Twist, and David Copperfield. The brilliant Dickens taps our deepest fears and hopes, not only with his characters who are children but also with his universal themes and his ability to make us care.

Whose writing sticks with you? Jot down a few lines to help you recall scenes from your favorite writers. What recurrent theme surfaces in the writing you hold dear?

Fanciful imagination born of a sense of wonder imprints itself upon my heart. I love Huck Finn's comments about living on a raft, looking at the sky speckled with stars, and Jim wondering if the moon laid them.

I savor the magic.

However you accomplish it, when your imagination soars, the fun of it all can be the cow's pajamas. Imagine how J.R.R. Tolkien felt creating Bilbo Baggins or how J.K. Rowling felt creating even one of her minor characters, such as Harry Potter's message owl, Hedwig.

There's a place where Hamlet, Cujo, Hannibal Lecter, Scarlett O'Hara, Elizabeth Bennet, and Maya Angelou's caged bird are all hanging out and singing together. But I don't know where.

I do know it's my inner Child who delights in the yellow-black butterfly sucking nectar from lavender phlox, who listens keenly to the cry of geese in the November sky, who is surprised by the sandpaper feel of a kitten's tongue when it licks milk from my finger. Emotion springs from the inner Child. Writers harvest armfuls of creative gifts from deep inside themselves. Make friends with the Kid and your writing will sing with feeling.

The inner Child isn't the actual child you once were; it's the child part of your personality that you have internalized and is under the care of your Adult and Parent ego states.

The field of psychotherapy known as transactional analysis (TA) brought the concept of ego states—Child, Adult, and Parent—into mainstream usage. Ego states are a theorized set of behaviors and ways of thinking and feeling. The words are capitalized to distinguish them from non-ego states. TA was developed by Eric Berne, M.D., who wrote *Games People Play*. Have you read or heard of the book, *I'm OK—You're OK* by Thomas A. Harris, M.D.? It's built on TA theory. Thinking about ego states can be a helpful tool for writers because the free inner Child is creative and has fun. The nurturing Parent takes care of you, especially your inner Child. The Adult is the rational part of your personality that churns out the work dispassionately. To write in an inspired way requires an integrated personality, a blend of Child-Adult-Parent ego states.

The Child has a strong will and is perfectly capable of thwarting Cecil the Critic as he pecks away at our self-esteem, but he or she needs our support. Discover what the Child needs by listening and do your best to meet those needs.

The Child plays, creates, relates to animals, and has certain wants "just because." If someone asks you, "Why do you want to do that?" and you find yourself answering, "I don't know, just because . . .," it's probably your Child doing the wanting.

Listen carefully. Sometimes the inner Child speaks in a very soft voice. Too often the real child was shamed for singing too loudly, or was rejected too many times, or got his hand slapped for not putting the crayons back properly when he was creating something. We carry those old feelings around and rerun them, but we don't have to. A free inner Child will express himself.

If you can find him.

Because your Child is vulnerable, you might have squirreled him away in a safe place and forgotten about him. If you keep your Child buried, you keep your emotions in check, but life will seem dull, and the pathways to your creativity could become blocked.

Now is a good time to think about the dreaded writer's block. If you find yourself blocked, check in with your Child to find out what's going on. Are you unsure how you feel? Ask. The Child knows. Fear and anger are killer blocks. Fear is such a biggie, it gets a chapter of its own. For now, let's consider anger.

Are you feeling trapped? Maybe you're working at a hated day job while your creative self is shaking the bars of her cage. Have you buried anger because life has laid an exhausting role as a caregiver at your feet? Anger becomes its own trap. Relaxation helps. Acceptance helps. Both can lead to salvaging bits of time for creative pursuits. Even a few minutes will feed your soul.

A reporter colleague of mine who doubled as a poet vowed, "They can't have all my stuff." At the end of the day, she kept a pocketful of energy back for her poems. Eventually heeding the siren song of poetry, she moved to Michigan's Upper Peninsula where she and her partner bought a bookstore on the shores of Lake Superior. I lost track of her, but I'd love to know whether she carved out more or less time for poetry. You have to chop a lot of wood to stay warm on Lake Superior. On the other hand, chopping wood may be an act of poetry.

If you're blocked, read. Actually, read as much as you can regardless. It's essential for writers to know what's being published in their genre, and there's always an opportunity to learn from the masters. Read and mull. If you challenge yourself with your reading, eventually you'll wind up writing your own words.

Your inner Child is a delightful partner in the creativity game. If you love creative writing, you're already hooked on that sense of wonder within, right? That's the essential you. Do you want to visit with him or her? Find out what's up? Do that with the meditation at the end of this chapter.

Some of us bury emotions such as pain, fear, and disappointment so they inhibit our inner Child. The Child can't trust us when we deny basic needs. Build trust. It's the foundation of creativity. If serious wounds hamper your inner Child, find competent, compassionate, professional help.

After the following inner Child meditation, one Moo workshop participant said, "That was powerful."

inner child meditation

Listen to Nan lead this meditation at nanlundeen.com.

Lie down or sit with your spine straight and your feet flat on the floor. Focus on your breath. Breathe slowly and deeply. Count silently. Breathe in: one—two—three—four. Breathe out: one—two—three—four. Breathe in: one—two—three—four. Breathe out: one—two—three—four. Continue breathing and counting. When thoughts intrude, let them drift by like fluffy clouds on a warm summer day. When you feel relaxed, call to mind a toy, a doll, a blanket, a favorite article of clothing or some other comforting object from your childhood. See your inner Child with that item. Kneel or sit beside him or her and have a conversation. When the two of you are finished talking, come back into the here and now.

writing exercises

- Continue physical exercise of your choice. While freewriting, draw or describe your inner Child.

- While freewriting, let your inner Child speak.

tips

- To write a memorable character, know him so well you know which arm he slips into his coat first. For your own use, write bios for your characters. Because emotion sits with each person in a Child persona, fully flesh out the childhood of each character in the bio. Even if you don't use all the information in your story, you will be writing with a viable backstory in mind. You'll write characters whose emotions are believable, whose motivations are understandable, and whose inconsistencies are appropriately baffling. Readers will identify with your characters and view them as multi-dimensional.

- Tap universal themes so that readers can identify with your story.

What do people truly care about?

Consider love, sex, money, romance, parents, children, mystery, coming of age, good and evil, self-actualization, and overcoming adversity. With good reason, some themes show up again and again—identity, for instance. Think of Luke Skywalker discovering more about himself when he learns that his father is Darth Vader.

moo notes

moo notes

moo notes

chapter 4
the boo of moo

Someone is ringing your doorbell. You hurry to answer it. Who stands there? You don't recognize him because he's masked. As if Halloween were a daily holiday, fear rings the doorbell, dressed in the mask of the moment, making impossible demands. Don't be fooled.

How might fear mask itself?

In an exercise at the end of this chapter, I invite you to sketch the face of your fear and name it.

Does that sound impossible? It will come easily, and the payoff is worth it. Recognize the face of your fear, and you've gained a valuable tool to help your creativity flow. First, identify the mask. Then, uncover the fear. Let me share my personal discovery with you as an example.

I sat down with a piece of paper and picked up two crayons that appealed to me in the moment, a red and a black. I breathed deeply and relaxed. I didn't think about it. Using the red crayon, I drew a longish rectangle that would become a face. Two black horizontal slits slashing across the page became eyes. The nose was a red, backwards comma, and a downward black arc cut short became a mouth.

When I looked at it, the name, "hopeless" popped into my mind. I could see that the partial mouth represented aborted self-expression. I labeled the drawing *hopeless and not entirely there.* The mask showed me that I'd been letting rejection slips get me down. Underneath the mask, fear said, *What's the use? The path ahead is strewn with rejections.*

The awareness made a huge difference in my life. I realized I'd been using fatigue and depression to mask my fear. Awareness is a great tool. It brought me new energy. "Hopeless" hangs around in my writing room as a reminder to be optimistic. He actually amuses me now, he's so pitiful.

Adding affirmations to your toolbox will help you build a more positive frame of mind. Did you create an affirmation in chapter 2 to address Cecil's concerns? Remember to keep affirmations short, positive, to the point, and in present tense. For instance, my affirmation to address "hopeless" is, *I choose hope.*

Repeat affirmations consistently if fear is scampering about in your brain with such messages as, *Is this good enough? Am I good enough? Will my wife, friends, mother, father, husband, children, online and print critics disapprove?*

Sometimes sharing our work feels like standing naked in front of a black-robed tribunal. We're probably fibbing to ourselves if we say we don't care what people think. Most of us care desperately because in our minds, our work is us.

So, we don masks to hide our fears from ourselves. We don't like to admit that fear could be an invisible driver in our lives. Masks are as tricky as a funhouse hall of mirrors. Procrastination, rationalization, and perfectionism make excellent masks, effective at disguising fear and tugging us away from writing. A little voice might nag us from beneath the mask, reminding us we really want to be writing now. But holy cow! We're good at ignoring that tiny whisper.

It's okay to be afraid. Just don't let fear paralyze you.

My mentor Sylvia Barclay advised that if a writer freezes when confronted by a blank page, she should begin writing anything. "If all you can write is the word, 'cat,' then begin," she said. "Write c-a-t over and over." Sylvia believed in establishing a habit of writing, and you can do that by daily freewriting as we discussed in chapter 2. If you tire of writing c-a-t, peek under your mask. Do you fear discovering something ugly about yourself?

What if underneath our masks, we are beautiful, and only the masks are ugly? Self-doubt and self-criticism are not only ugly, they're a waste of time. Some writers feel vulnerable; some are shy. A Moo workshop writer shared that she fears looking foolish. From time to time, we lose faith in ourselves. Not to worry. Faith like a recurring musical theme will return.

It is foolish, however, to write from a position of ignorance. Moo is about getting your creativity flowing, but if you want to produce credible work, build on a foundation of knowledge. Not everybody can or wants to take college-level courses or earn college degrees. If that is your goal, go for it! If not, find other ways to research, study, and learn. Consider online classes, local workshops, and how-to-write books and magazines. Brush up on point of view, story structure, grammar and spelling, what a cliché is, and how to build a good sentence. If you're a poet, study the various forms of poetry and practice composing them. Study master poets. Read widely in your genre.

Research your topic thoroughly, especially when writing nonfiction, but don't use research as a means to avoid writing.

You may find information in *Moo of Writing* you disagree with, but I hope you won't find the author's ignorance blithely displayed. (No guarantees, though.) For instance, I had been advising Moo workshop writers to write haiku as an exercise to sharpen their awareness. I defined haiku as a three-line poem, the form having originated in Japan, that took a five-seven-five syllable form, usually on the subject of nature, often with a seasonal theme.

Fortunately, one day when I was hanging out at Folly Beach, South Carolina, with a group of women friends, I was musing about a yellow flower blooming by the steps and forming a haiku about it. My friend Maggie recommended *The Haiku Handbook: How to Write, Teach, and Appreciate Haiku* by William J. Higginson and Penny Harter. I ordered the book upon my return home and found it to be stellar. I learned that the art form is highly nuanced and not dependent on seventeen-syllable construction. In fact, twelve more accurately translate from the Japanese; however, literality isn't necessary. You can experiment with free-form, and overall, aspects other than syllable count may be more important. But, writing five-seven-five syllable poems is fun and an excellent exercise. If you want to delve into the art form, read the book or visit the websites of haiku organizations such as Haiku Society of America. That will be fun, too. Either way, you can observe your world and write haiku in your head while you're going for your Moo walk.

I love writing because the challenge is endless. There's always more to learn. Education helps build self-confidence so that you become an authoritative writer.

Rather than letting yourself be driven by hidden fears, find your balance. Do that by searching for and discovering antidotes that work for you. Everyone is different; have fun with your search.

Education definitely will help.

Pleasure also provides an excellent antidote. Indulge in doses of pleasure every day, something to make your inner Child happy. When embodied in a writer, the inner Child has much work to do, and must be given regular treats. When she's happy, she's not feeding hidden fears.

To cope with fear, New Age practitioners including Louise Hay, Shakti Gawain, and others recommend mentally creating a safe place. Being an Iowa native, mine is a warm, red barn. Would your inner Child enjoy a respite? Enjoy the Safe Space Meditation at the end of this chapter.

When fear in one guise or another berates me, earth calms me. Digging in dirt, doing chores in the yard, and listening to birds and squirrels help to dispel that old bugaboo.

May Sarton, twentieth century New England poet, novelist, and journal writer, loved to garden, and turning over earth, found poems growing there. It's good to incorporate at least a few minutes of grounding pastime into each day, even if it's polishing the teakettle, which is what Israeli Premier Golda Meir did when she faced stress.

If you're stressed out, even if you can do nothing else, remember to take deep breaths. Deep breathing will ease you.

Another antidote—imagine picking up your anxiety and putting it in a box. It won't go away, but your path will clear.

Writing prompts are a great little tool when fear blocks you and even when it doesn't. They abound online. One coming in daily via an email newsletter for writers provides a nice backup if your creativity is stuck but wants to meander in the meadow.

Writing a description of your fear will help. Try incorporating that into your freewriting. You'll discover underlying fears that benefit from the light. Once you've unmasked them, compose affirmations to address them.

Don't be hoodwinked. Unmask. Stare fear in the eye.

Once you've recognized your fear, accept it and determine to keep writing. Determination isn't a set jaw. Determination is writing the next sentence. It's pondering who your fictional character's parents were. Where did your character grow up? What is the rhythm of his voice? What metaphor would work for the poem you are gestating? Set your mind to these thoughts even though fear disguised by masks sets whirligigs spinning in your head.

Breathe and keep writing.

Completed bodies of work will reward you. They are as lively as a purple iris blooming happily in the garden and as much to be savored as a golden loaf of bread fresh from the oven.

Are rewards what it's all about?

At heart, or at gut, we're kids. And kids love rewards. Writing is solitary, and gratification can be so delayed that writing could be the granddaddy of self-flagellation. Or, you could become successful and be tortured by your number one fan, as was Paul Sheldon in Stephen King's novel, *Misery.*

What rewards your writing? Traditionally, we think of money and recognition.

Scratch those. They might happen. They might not.

A relaxed writer avoids lashing her tail in a frenzy. She definitely doesn't worry about what price her five gallons of milk per day will bring at market.

The reward of writing is writing. It's the process. It's the rumination and the artistic expression. For most of us, it sure isn't the power and the glory. When you achieve one good sentence, however, you can honestly say, *amen.*

safe space meditation

Listen to Nan lead this meditation at nanlundeen.com.

Get comfortable. Curl up in a cozy chair or on a couch. Pull a favorite blanket, afghan, or comforter around you. Or sit outdoors, any place at all you feel at ease. Focus on your breath. Breathe slowly and deeply. Count silently. Breathe in: one—two—three—four. Breathe out: one—two—three—four. Breathe in: one—two—three—four. Breathe out: one—two—three—four. Continue breathing and counting. Let your thoughts meander like dreams. Breathe. Relax. All is well. Breathe deeply and remember a place where you felt completely safe. It could have been at any time in your life. Breathe. Relax. All is well. Are you remembering a special place? A person who held you? A time when you experienced spiritual comfort? Experience again the feeling of safety. Relax into it. Drop your guard. Breathe. If you wish, create a new place in your mind where you feel safe. Know that you can visit your safe space at any time if only for a few moments. When you feel ready, open your eyes and come back into the here and now.

writing exercises

- Continue daily physical exercise of your choice and free-writing.

- Gather drawing tools. Use whatever you have on hand such as, crayons, pencils, markers, colored pencils, scrap paper, or sketch paper. If you're comfortable with a drawing program on your tablet or computer, use it. Relax and use the Safe Space Meditation from this chapter. Ask your fear to appear in your mind. Without thinking, draw or sketch your fear. Name it.

- Write an affirmation to resolve your fear. Make it short, specific, and in the present tense. Examples: *I acknowledge my fear of_____ and move forward.* Or, *I write even when I feel fearful.* Or, *fear, I recognize you behind that mask of_____. I enjoy writing.*

- Write a letter to your inner Child describing how you are creating safe writing space for him or her. End with an affirmation.

tips

- When writing fiction, consider imagining your main characters first. When you have created solid characters, the story will follow. Have fun examining favorite characters from literature and think about why they appeal to you. I love Scout Finch, the Little Prince, and the voice in Robert Frost's poem, "Stopping by Woods on a Snowy Evening."

- When writing memoir, set it in context with events of the times to establish a means for your readers to connect with you. What was happening in the world that was important to you? Global warming? The 2004 Indian Ocean tsunami that struck the coastlines of eleven countries, leaving millions homeless? The election of Barack Obama, the first U.S. black president?

moo notes

moo notes

moo notes

chapter 5
listen up! this is your gut speaking

Writers need courage. In my workshops, I've noticed that a lack of self-esteem and self-confidence pester writers who struggle with the craft. Now and again, these writers give me a glimpse of the wonderful stories and poems that lie within their souls and want to come out. Actually, all of us require a daily dose of courage, rather like Roo's strengthening medicine in Winnie the Pooh stories. Summoning courage when you're short on self-esteem can exhaust you.

You can hone your craft through study, hard work, and application. Mentors, editors, educators, and other writers will help a great deal, but to write in your authentic voice with authority requires a close relationship with your gut.

Billions of people live on this planet, yet each of us is unique. That's astounding! Rather than conforming to others' expectations, a self-actualized writer hearkens to his or her individuality.

The belly is a wise old soul. Some say it has a mind of its own. While intuition resides in a "sixth sense" or as some believe, on a spiritual plane, it also houses itself in ample amounts in the gut.

In chapter 3, you made friends with your inner Child, a boundless source of emotion and creativity. Deepen that growing friendship by listening to your gut. Strength and self-esteem lie there. Write from your center—your place of power—and hidden fears cannot drive you.

How do you tap into gut power?

Cultivate your third chakra.

The word "chakra" comes from the Sanskrit language of India and means "wheel." The tradition teaches that the seven major chakras are spinning vortexes of energy or wheels of light arranged vertically from the base of the spine to the top of the head, governing physical, earthy energies at the base and progressing to spiritual energies at the top, or seventh chakra.

The energy of the core self spins in the third chakra located at the solar plexus (between the belly button and the bottom of the rib cage). It involves the digestion of life experiences and the application of personal power. Each chakra is associated with a color. The third chakra's color is yellow.

Writers, like cows, require superb digestive systems. Woefully short of the four stomach compartments cows are blessed with, writers, nonetheless, are forever chewing on life experiences. Much of that energy work goes on in the third chakra.

To harness the energies life dishes up for us—to put them to use and be active, not passive, requires a strong sense of self and more than a dollop of ambition. Self-esteem and strength of character revolve around the third chakra.

What is your vision of a writer with healthy self-esteem?

I see a person who has fun writing, rather than feeling driven to prove himself, someone with the discipline to keep to a writing schedule and submit work often, and who remains calm and focused even if he receives harsh criticism. A person with healthy self-esteem respects other writers, letting envy and jealousy find a home elsewhere rather than in his own heart. He stays the course because he feels confident.

Take a moment or two to create affirmations that address third chakra energies. My affirmation: *I choose to bring my work to full completion.*

Think of listening to your gut as checking in with your intuition. Best buddies, creativity and intuition wander through pastures side by side. When you use intuition, you know something without applying reason. You *feel* it. A mind of its own implies a will, as well. Have you ever fought against your "gut instincts?" I have, and it's gut-wrenching. Not only that, my rational side never wins. I might do the rational thing, but if I persevere even when it *feels* wrong, my gut will serve up misery in heaping spoonfuls.

Necessity requires us to fulfill some of the expectations that society and we, ourselves, place upon us, but not all. Earning a living so that we can pay the bills ranks way up there and forces us to fulfill others' expectations and our own sense of responsibility. If you're in a job that you hate, and it demands all your time and energy, leaving nothing for creative pursuits, consider a practical, realistic change. What does your gut tell you? Do you want to find work that is more satisfying? Could your present job transition into that? Finding time to write can be a struggle. We'll address that issue in chapter 7 when we discuss how to befriend time. For now, think about how to balance necessary expectations with your creative pursuits.

There are many romantic stories of how some writers quit their day jobs, living hand-to-mouth, going without medicine for their kids, and other unacceptable sacrifices to fully invest their time in their writing. Just when they thought all was lost, boom! A book contract came through. I don't recommend that kind of risk. Be realistic. Few authors earn a living wage even with the dreamed-of book contract.

The creative force takes a multitude of forms from the arts to business to raising great kids. Ask yourself: *when do I feel the most creative?*

I find that words and ideas often flow most easily when I'm doing something else, sort of coming at it sideways, such as playing the piano or drawing a bird with colored pencils or taking a break from a work in progress to wash dishes. Creativity operates somewhere else in my consciousness like background noise. That's the mind-wandering aspect of creativity we discussed in chapter 1.

Maya Angelou was quoted by several news media saying that her grandmother spoke of a "little mind." The story goes that when she was a child, Angelou decided she had a Little Mind and a Big Mind. The Little Mind would be caught up in the day-by-day, and the Big Mind would be occupied with deep thoughts. Angelou kept a hotel room where she would retire from the world to write. She kept her Little Mind occupied with crosswords or a game of solitaire so that her Big Mind could be free to express itself. She wrote from 6:30 a.m. until about 1 p.m. and then went home and edited.

Mind-body healing gurus tell us that the confidence to manifest our intentions and desires involves energy freely flowing through the third chakra. When that energy is blocked, we feel powerless and frustrated.

If you get stuck on a piece of writing, take a nap. This suggestion shocked a colleague. She wanted to know if I meant this literally, or if I meant "take a break." Yes, I mean it literally. If you sleep with creativity on your pillow, you will wake up with ideas floating to the forefront. Rested, you will produce quality work. Fatigued, you will merely work.

Many of us use the phrase, "my gut feeling is (whatever)." Our gut doesn't always talk sense from the perspective of our logical minds, and the feelings may not fit with our shoulds. Nevertheless, if you go with your gut, you are hearkening to a deep, inner wisdom. Imagine the personal power you tap into when you listen to your gut—expectations that make you miserable fizzle.

Your gut reveals motivations indigenous to you.

To act upon them is to be who you choose to be.

belly meditation

Listen to Nan lead this meditation at nanlundeen.com.

Lie down or sit with your spine straight and your feet
flat on the floor. Place your palm on your belly between
your belly button and the bottom of your ribs. Focus
on your breath. Breathe slowly and deeply. Breathe in:
one—two—three—four. Breathe out: one—two—
three—four. Breathe in: one—two—three—four. Breathe
out: one—two—three—four. Continue breathing and
counting. When thoughts intrude, let them drift by like
fluffy clouds on a warm summer day. Take a deep breath.
Imagine a golden light glowing under your hand. Imagine
it growing. Imagine it radiating from you like spokes from
a warm sun. Breathe. Don't try to accomplish anything
with this meditation. Simply be. When you are ready,
open your eyes and return to the here and now.

writing exercises

- Continue physical exercise of your choice. For as long as it feels good to you, do the belly meditation (above) before daily freewriting.

- Write a love note to your belly, describing how much you admire it and why. Praise its attributes. Then, using your non-dominant hand, write a love note to yourself from your belly. Let your belly describe how much it admires you and why. Praise your attributes.

tips

- You've enlisted your gut in the service of your writing, now how about your ear? A writer needs a good ear as much as a musician does. Read your work aloud and listen carefully. If you get a gut feeling—no matter how fleeting or subdued—that something isn't quite right, read it aloud again and imagine someone listening. Pay attention to mood, voice, rhythms, diction, and attitude. Be alert to anything that jars the ear, anything that nudges you. Does it need changing?

- Entertain yourself writing. Do your words make you laugh? Bring tears to your eyes? Make you think, wow? That's what you're after. If your words are a drudge to drag yourself through, think how horribly they'll bore a reader. Go for a belly laugh.

moo notes

moo notes

chapter 6
moo stone

To implement belly wisdom, write from your center. Power lies in the writing process because you are synthesizing all that you are and all that you know into art.

Synthesizing can feel overwhelming. Some creative people, given their propensity to soak up huge amounts of stimuli, feel scattered. Words flit about in their heads like butterflies, and they follow swarms of alluring wings down garden paths to incoherency.

Good writing requires focus. We want to avoid wasting our lives chewing cud without producing much except cow pies.

Practicing a belly meditation, such as the one offered at the end of the previous chapter, carries you well on your way to a centering practice, a practice that will engender self-confidence.

I like to use an additional tool—a Moo stone. My stone is round, speckled, three inches across, and about one-half inch thick. If you choose to try this practice, search for a stone that appeals to your eye, but most important, find one that feels good in your hand.

You'll find a Moo stone meditation at the end of this chapter. I hope it beckons you. It's the most important of the meditations I'm sharing with you.

I encourage you to meditate with your Moo stone daily. The practice is most effective just before freewriting. Set a minimum amount of time that you will do this at first until you begin to sense on your own that you've connected with what you need. Store your Moo stone in a resting spot near a comfortable chair. This is the only meditation I recommend that you do daily. The others can be done as you read along in this handbook; they can be returned to and re-experienced any time.

I find a stone comforting and real, but there's no need to be rigid about how you center yourself. Use whatever works for you.

South Carolina fiction writer Josette Davison says, "My centering stone is the sound of the train whistle at night, which takes me immediately back to my childhood bed in a tiny pottery town in Ohio. That was where I first yearned to use words to express my deepest feelings."

At your center lies your true self. No matter what you write, no matter what your genre, good writing originates there. Writing pundits like to carry on about "finding your voice." Your voice resides at your center. Your voice is the Moo of you.

First, build a foundation by clarifying why you want to write. It could be something as simple as, *because it's what I do*. Keep in mind, it may change over time.

If you want to write romance novels for money, for instance, study the genre, target your market, and write away!

If you're a poet, read contemporary poets and decide what type of poet you want to be. Are you a populist? An academic? A humorist? A satirist? A blend? Do you want your work to be accessible? Do you place importance on recognition by top-ranking literary journals and magazines?

It's good to know why you want to write because the why comes first, then the what. Be clear.

Moo workshop writer Jackie Weddington says, "I write what I see, what I read about, what I know to be true. About living and dying, joy and sorrow, children, and my mother's hands are mine, now. The men who can't come in out of the rain, the poet who died in a graveyard drowned in a moonlit sea, about women and children, fear and darkness, falling down and getting up, about glory and age. Beauty. I write about life as being a gift no matter how difficult."

James A. Fisher, a former member of my critique group, says, "I enjoy writing for my own amusement and amazement, for the pure lark of it."

Writer Jenny Munro says, "I write to stay alive. Without the words coming out, I feel dead. And the interesting thing is that it doesn't matter what I write—journalism, creative, memoir. Anything that connects my brain, my heart, my eyes, and my hands works."

Once you know why you write, how do you summon your power?

You've read much in this handbook about feelings, but now it's time to set your feelings aside. You can't write effectively when you're clutching in fear or weeping empathetic tears or soothing some part of your personality in desperate need.

You do need emotion to create memorable writing, but come to the page with almost a cold self-confidence. You've done your relaxations, your freewriting, and your meditations. You've explored and dreamed and day-dreamed. You've read and you've thought and you've ruminated. Now, center yourself so that the wordsmith takes over. Write with precision from an integrated mind. You are whole, and the unsentimental, tough part of you must come to the fore.

Earlier, I shared with you images from a poem I wrote about my father appearing at woods' edge carrying buckets of blackberries when I was about two. I struggled with the tone of that poem for years, couldn't make it past sentimentality, wasn't conveying emotion with a dispassionate pen.

Finally, the appropriate tone hit me:

> is this your new job
> now that you're dead—
> strewing bucketsful of stars
> along the Wapsi?

I had the beginning. When you detach and write from a synthesized point, you will strike the tone that fits whatever you are working on and that suits your voice.

Have you watched a potter at his wheel or thrown a pot yourself? Synthesizing your powers to shape a piece of writing is like throwing a pot. You've chosen a chunk of clay, clay of a certain texture and a certain size. You've kneaded it and incorporated water. You've rounded it and visualized a form. Finally, you pitch the clay onto the wheel and cup your hands around it. The wheel spins. You work in harmony with it.

As the wheel of time turns, we no longer know whether we are shaping the work or the work is shaping us.

Buddhist teacher Thich Nhat Hanh relates a story about writing in his book, *Anger*. The celebrated poet shares that an American Buddhist scholar asked why he doesn't spend more time writing his beautiful poems rather than on tasks such as growing lettuce.

For Thich Nhat Hanh, it is through daily tasks done with mindfulness that poetry comes.

Mu.

Or, Moo.

As we practice Moo, our work lies there in the clay, waiting to be formed. When you center yourself, you make peace with yourself—rooted like an oak tree, you can weather many storms.

I have a long way to go to reach the detachment I long for, and my emotions can still pitch me into turbulent waters, but I spend less time flailing about than I used to. I process the feelings and come into calm waters more quickly. I hope with practice, I'll be able to believe when I'm in turmoil that calm waters await me.

I keep Jesus' words as written in John 14:27 on my home altar: "Peace I leave with you; my peace I give you. I do not give to you as the world gives. Do not let your hearts be troubled and do not be afraid."

I sometimes talk to my Moo stone: Good, round stone, you are my best friend because you are me and because you are at the same time my companion. But who are you, really? Are you the crow that croaks like a frog I hear in the woods outside my window? Are you the two hawks I was amazed to see land on our neighbor's lawn? Are you the center of the cloud that mars the sun as if it were too lonely to go on? Some days, I think you are my heart.

Friends, I don't know what else to share with you about Moo stones except I hope you find yourself one.

moo stone meditation

Listen to Nan lead this meditation at nanlundeen.com.

Sit with your spine straight and your feet flat on the floor. Hold your Moo stone in one hand resting in your lap and breathe deeply. Count silently. Breathe in: one—two—three—four. Breathe out: one—two—three—four. Breathe in: one—two—three—four. Breathe out: one—two—three—four. Continue breathing and counting. When thoughts intrude, let them drift by like fluffy clouds on a warm summer day. Imagine energy flowing down from the stone through your feet deep into Mother Earth. Breathe. Leave your energy down there for a few breaths. Now, draw the energy up, up, up to shower over your head like a fountain and then deep into Mother Earth again. Repeat as long as you wish. When you are ready, come back into the here and now. Set your stone in its resting place and return to it tomorrow. Peace.

writing exercises

- Continue daily physical exercise of your choice and freewriting. Begin a daily Moo stone meditation. So far, you've been writing on whatever subjects appear on the page after relaxation. Now, let's try something new. Let's try focused freewriting. Following your Moo stone meditation, choose a topic and write freely while staying on the topic. For instance, you may decide to write freely on a work in progress. Choose a specific spot in your work that you want to open up with freewriting. Is there a part of your work that needs a breath of fresh air? Write for ten minutes letting words flow, but stick to the topic. If you're writing fiction, stay in the point of view and/or in the character's voice. If you're writing poetry, expand, expand. Let the words flow without internal editing, letting the lines break wherever they wish. Don't think, now I need a metaphor or a good simile. Just step into the flow. With poetry, your pen may veer off topic. That's okay. Let the words wander. You may discover wild connections you can rework later. Stay inside the poem, but don't think. Mu.

- Write on the subject: I write because . . .

tips

- Stay on topic. Everything included in the piece must apply to the subject at hand.

- Be specific. Employ the red-boot method. An editor at a newspaper where I worked used to regale us with a story illustrating the importance of using the right detail. Especially in newspaper stories, writers must be succinct; therefore, details carry a heavy burden. A reporter had been given the sad assignment of writing about a little girl's death. When she visited the girl's home, the journalist noticed a pair of small, red boots sitting on the front porch next to the door. She placed that detail in her story. It was worth more than a thousand words.

- Fully actualize your vision on the page. Help the reader see the scene as it plays in your head. Do the words present a full, nuanced picture? The reader only sees what you put on the page; he cannot read your mind. For instance, in a poem mentioning my eventual death and burial in my native Iowa, I wrote:

> I'll return soon enough for my planting there
> alongside Louie and Marian and a swan
> in Clinton Memorial Gardens.

In my mind, I saw the swan that swims sedately in the pond near my parents' graves. My critique group asked why a swan was buried next to my parents.

moo notes

moo notes

moo notes

chapter 7
befriend time

If you focus on lack of writing time, you will soon have none. If you focus on available writing time, even if it's only ten minutes a day, you'll be surprised how much you will accomplish. If you make time your enemy, you'll run about hurried and harried, trying to finish everything else before you allow yourself to sit down and write. Your attitude will be, *there aren't enough hours in the day!*

Choose to think of time not as an enemy holding a club over your head arbitrarily ruling how you must spend your minutes and hours, but as a warm friendly animal, a loving companion.

Time loves to be cuddled, appreciated, and scratched behind the ear. Time will return kindness with kindness. Mistreat him, and he will scurry away, scowl, and hide in a corner. If provoked, he may bite.

He needs a friend as much as you or I.

Realistically, it takes a good bit of sorting to befriend time. It takes practice, permission, and positive thinking.

In 1980, I was a single mom in Holland, Michigan, and had saved my pennies to take my eleven-year-old daughter Jennifer on a trip to New York. We had set a time to meet our friend Minnie and her friend Charles at a Midtown sidewalk cafe. When Jennifer and I arrived, Charles was already there. The city bustled in the background as we introduced ourselves and waited for Minnie. Our new acquaintance, an actor and director, had an uncanny way of reading people. He decided upon meeting me that I was a strong woman, and that I was dedicated to my job as a newspaper reporter.

"I'll bet you read newspapers on your time off, am I right?"

I laughed and launched into my frustration that there wasn't enough time in my day to do creative writing.

Charles advised, "Befriend time."

Whoa! Stop the presses! I hearkened back to a decade earlier when Sylvia, my writing mentor, advised that if you could eke out only ten minutes each day for your writing, do so. Be realistic about time, she advised. Had I taken her advice? No, I spent at least ten minutes every day fueling my frustrations over my lack of time to write.

I remembered reading an article in a writers' magazine about a mother of a passel of kids who wrote a book out of the back of her station wagon (pre-SUV era) when she chauffeured kids to Little League games and who knows where else. I hated that woman. How dare she find time to write under those circumstances? How dare she be able to focus? When I think about her now after all these years, I realize her attitude must have been light. She couldn't have taken herself too seriously; instead, she was having fun. She wasn't moaning with the back of her hand to her forehead, "Oh, God, when will I have time to write?" She was down-to-earth and practical and couldn't be bothered with suffering over her writing.

In chapter 2, we talked about spending a set amount of time on daily freewriting. Some folks call that discipline. That's okay, or you could think of it as practice. Building any skill requires repetition. For instance, people can learn to master their emotions by practicing deep breathing regularly. If an emotion threatens to overwhelm you, your practice will come to the rescue because you'll remember to take deep breaths. If you haven't been practicing, you could dive into turmoil. Your practice will make space for peace in your life.

Befriending time takes practice, also. Be patient with yourself.

A friend who wants to write said, "That ten-minutes-a-day thing doesn't work for me. When I sit down to write, I don't even get started in ten minutes. But when I do start, the words just flow and I could write for hours."

My friend works full time outside the home, and her husband travels a great deal for his job. They have kids in middle school. Children, of course, deserve an abundance of love and nurturing which takes time.

Her incomplete mystery novel languishes because she can't stick with it as long as she wants. So, she's doing no writing. Zip. Zero. Maybe the novel won't materialize at this time in her life. Her life circumstances and method of writing may not permit her to finish it now. Some writers can create a novel in short spurts; others require chunks of time at one sitting. Writing charms us into losing ourselves. We love to be "somewhere else" in our imagination. That's why people love to read, too. Have you read late into the night and been shocked when you looked at a clock?

Time scowls at rigidity. Maybe my friend could make peace with alternatives for now and could steal whole hours whenever possible. Would she try haiku, or four lines in her journal, or flash fiction? When she returns to the novel some day, she would have practiced writing succinctly with simplicity. Can't hurt.

If she chooses to stick with the novel, she would have to sacrifice sleep which could result in rabbit-hole experiences of unwelcome consequences, although that depends upon her constitution. A colleague of mine wrote short stories and a novel while raising kids and working outside the home by getting up at four a.m. every day to write. If stealing time from sleep in the morning or at night doesn't work, and a writer keeps struggling and remains frustrated no matter her best intentions, resentment will take up residence in her soul, causing pain for herself and her family.

If you're a stay-at-home mom or dad with small children, consider finding a group of writers in the same circumstance and trade off playdates. You'll gain time and space to write, and you'll be helping other writers.

To befriend time, it's imperative to be flexible and to sidestep frustration. Experiment to see what works for you. To begin, become aware of how you think and feel about time.

Is time your enemy? Are you hurried and harried? Spend a few moments in relaxation or meditation to conjure up your image of time. Mine probably would be that grim reaper guy with the scythe because I'm past seventy now, and want to write, write, write so many things before I die.

I need an affirmation. I think I'll try, *I have as much time as I need to write right now.* Ecclesiastes 3:1 is comforting to repeat: "There is a time for everything, and a season for every activity under heaven."

If you're frustrated with time, you could use it as fodder for a poem or story about frustration. Frustration provides a ready-made conflict that will fuel a plot. Let your imagination run with it. What else other than time might supremely frustrate a fictional character? Is he thwarted at every turn? Empathize with your character. Throw up wall after wall. You know how he feels. Write that. His ultimate triumph will be sweet.

A Moo workshop writer shared that she could squeeze fifteen minutes of freewriting into her day, but she couldn't make an appointment with herself because her work schedule was erratic. Her workshop colleagues brainstormed an affirmation that would encourage her: *Every day, I am flexible to claim fifteen minutes for relaxation and freewriting.* They suggested that a photo, a drawing, or some other form of art would provide a "double whammy," a visual as well as a written reminder. Affirmations are wonderfully supportive tools that serve not only as reminders, but also as permission.

A friend named Rae who wrote, edited a magazine, and was a single mom, said that because she recognized her time was important, she scheduled her days and went to bed early. Realizing that your <u>time</u> is important means you realize <u>you</u> are important. Rae gave herself permission to write her own stuff and scheduled it into her day. She was realistic and didn't set it as a priority above her work or her parenting; neither did she sacrifice it.

Weigh other peoples' requests for your time and energy thoughtfully. Avoid a knee-jerk response of "yes" when someone asks for a chunk of your time. Give yourself a day or two to consider the request. It's good to be kind and generous to others, and it's also good to be kind and generous to yourself. It's okay to say no. Do you consider other peoples' needs more important than your own? Your writing time is important. You needn't put your time on a throne and worship it, but neither should you put it last. Be gentle with yourself. Love yourself.

If you love to write and are writing full time, rejoice!

To be productive, some writers set deadlines. For instance, if you decide to provide your writers' critique group with a certain output by a scheduled time, hooray! There's your ready-made goal.

A task will expand to fill available time even if it steals time from writing. Better that your writing play the role of thief rather than victim. Do you want to make writing a top priority, secondary only to necessary tasks? For instance, if your dog won't do his business in the yard, to prevent accidents in the house, he must be walked first thing. Then, writing is the next priority of the day. If you're at home with little ones, writing is a top priority when they're down for a nap or tucked in for the night. The laundry won't evaporate. It will wait patiently.

Be careful that your lack of writing time isn't fear hiding behind a mask. Are you using a perceived lack of time as an excuse not to write?

Whining consumes time and energy. Better to invest in thinking about the plot of your next novel, the title of the personal essay you're gestating, or a line of poetry. It's like sitting at the kitchen table over your second cup of coffee thinking, *how am I ever going to find time to exercise,* rather than pushing your chair back, opening the door, and going for a walk. When something needed doing, my mother, who was a schoolteacher, used to say, "There's no time like the present!"

Still, many writers struggle because they have a day job. Here's where my mentor Sylvia's advice to be realistic about how much time you can devote to your writing applies. Settle for whatever bits of time you can squeeze out. I struggled for many years even after Charles shared his wisdom about befriending time. I wrote a whole lot as a reporter and couldn't even read in the evening when my eyes were tired and my brain was surfeited with words. I gave myself the pleasure of writing four lines in my journal every day. Four lines. I had fun letting my mind wander to the lines I would write. Best of all, they were mine. They belonged to no editor, no publication. People who write for a living whether in journalism or other fields have similar issues. Jobs in any field present their own stresses and demands.

Take what you can get wherever, whenever. It's vital to seize the time you do have. You're alive. You're breathing. Write four lines today if that's all you can do. Schedule an hour on your day off. Keep a notebook handy in the bathroom. Grab the time that you have. Relax into it. Be its friend. Sow seeds of writing happiness. Fulfilling your desire to write will make you a happier person, and you'll have more time and energy for other tasks rather than resenting them. Decide how much time you want to devote to other tasks. Prioritize. If non-writing tasks overwhelm your schedule, what will you cut?

Give yourself permission to write.

We're hard-wired to be creatures of habit. The rhythms of life comfort us just as we were comforted—if we were lucky—when we were held and rocked as infants. Have fun discovering your innate output rhythms and use them as guides. Some writers naturally produce two pages daily while others churn out a whole chapter. Some might labor over a book for ten years while others roll out two a year. Are you a night owl? An early riser? Harness your natural tendencies.

Do you like to focus on one project at a time? Or do you like to rotate your focus: today I'll write this, tomorrow that, the third day something else, then back to the first again? Settling into a rhythm keeps your words flowing.

A word about distractions—they gobble up time in relentless small bites. Do you sit down to write only to first check your email, social media posts, favorite blogs, news websites, on and on? We're creatures of habit, and distractions can be addictive. But we're also creatures with free will. Choose whether to begin writing when you sit down to commune with your muse or choose to quickly check the latest email, which will, of course, lead you down a diversionary path, which will, of course, lead you down a second diversionary path and into the woods of no return.

To befriend time, be gentle with yourself. Keep your goals flexible lest you rebel. Time is life. When you love yourself you are befriending time.

At this chapter's beginning, I wrote, "Choose to think of time not as an enemy holding a club over your head arbitrarily ruling how you must spend your minutes and hours, but as a warm friendly animal, a loving companion." I'm repeating it here because I want you to pay attention to the word, "choose." Finding time to write is a matter of choice. Any other behavior is passive. Writers have eked out words on toilet paper in prison cells. How important is your writing to you? If it's just a now-and-then pastime, fine. If it's more, make friends with time. Minutes and hours are ticks of the heart.

Do you see that none of this happens without a positive attitude? Shift your way of thinking about time. If you choose, you can meditate on your attitude, or you can ask your higher power for help in achieving it, or you can read self-help books, or take a course. Writing in your journal will help and so will affirmations unique to you. Search for your own way of cultivating the positive. Adopting a positive attitude is the most important thing you will ever do.

"Those who wish to sing always find a song." – Swedish proverb.

cloud meditation

Listen to Nan lead this meditation at nanlundeen.com.

Lie down or sit with your spine straight and your feet flat on the floor. Focus on your breath. Breathe slowly and deeply. Count silently. Breathe in: one—two—three—four. Breathe out: one—two—three—four. Breathe in: one—two—three—four. Breathe out: one—two—three—four. Continue breathing and counting. When thoughts intrude, let them drift by like fluffy clouds on a warm summer day. When you feel relaxed, imagine yourself lying on a grassy hillside on a warm, breezy day. Look up at the sky. As you continue deep breathing, notice the clouds. What color are they? What shapes? As you observe, notice that one of them is taking a shape that expresses your feelings about time. Does it hold that shape, or does it change? Observe. When you are ready, open your eyes and come back to the here and now.

writing exercises

- Continue physical exercise of your choice, daily Moo stone meditation, and freewriting.

- Describe the image of time you perceived in the above meditation. Let time speak on the page.

- Write an affirmation to express how you befriend time. Place copies of it where it will benefit you.

- Pretend nothing exists but this moment. Describe where you are and what you are feeling now.

tips

- Language that uses positive statements is stronger than negative wordage. William Strunk Jr. and E.B. White advise in their classic book, *The Elements of Style*, to cast statements in a positive form. That works for any genre. They advise never to use the word *not* as a "means of evasion." Evasive language is wishy-washy. For instance, it's more interesting to say somebody is "strolling down the road" rather than "he's not moving very fast."

- Time will befriend your manuscript. Let it rest at least overnight, and preferably a few days or much longer. When you come back to it, you'll read it with a fresh perspective, and what needs to be changed will come clear.

- Beg, barter, or negotiate a writer's retreat time for yourself as often as you can. Make it a place of solitude.

moo notes

moo notes

chapter 8
play's the thing

I have a hunch that Sophia, the goddess of wisdom, looks with tenderness upon us humans who take life so seriously. At times, life slaps us in the face with awful, unavoidable stuff; at times, we feel joy; at other times, we just muddle along.

Lift your spirit with buoyant words.

Does your muse indulge in humor? In your dreams, do you find a pun or two? The subconscious and maybe the spirit world appreciate humor, never derisive or harmful, simply fun.

The creative process carries many graces, among them fun, catharsis, inspiration, and satisfaction. A Moo workshop participant says she writes because she loves to tell stories. She has distilled her motivation into something joyful. Some of us tend to be hard on ourselves, even puritanical, so we pour art into our life's forge and hammer the creative process into suffering. Suffering already exists in sufficient amounts, don't you think?

But, what if a gut-wrenching subject commands our pens?

Writers grapple with the human condition. Death and suffering—in what my childhood minister called "this vale of tears"—is fodder for great literature, such as Victor Hugo's *Les Miserables*. Many wonderful writers choose to stare pain in the eye. The result? Beauty, perhaps, and almost always, a dollop of solace in the sharing for both the writer and the reader.

In his book, *The Time I Didn't Know What To Do Next*, contemporary poet J. Stephen Rhodes writes about his daughter's suicide. His poems reveal grace and strength from a position of grief.

Life is a mixed bag, joyful and sorrowful and occasionally just blah. Our society, however, tends to look at things from an either-or-construct, such as happy or sad, work or play. Dualistic thinking dries up creativity. Reject the work-play dichotomy. Work is play and play is work, and often the twain will meet.

Now and again, when I'm writing, I'll laugh out loud, and my husband will call from the other room, "Amusing yourself again?"

Indeed.

Every so often, a writer feels as if he or she has tapped a fount that pulses like life itself. Those are precious writing moments, and even if they only come seldom, they bless our work and keep it flowing.

Can you write serious things playfully?

It's a matter of perspective. Try taking a light attitude, letting the words flow to a tune of their own. Language has a talent that way. When you read a superbly written book, do you savor each word? The written word can bless us with pleasure in the reading and in the writing even when it's about sad things. Satisfaction comes from excellence of self-expression.

Let us get together and celebrate our written words. Let us break open the champagne and get stinko together. Let us pound one another on the back and say, "Well done."

If you don't have anybody to do that with, please find somebody.

I Love To meditation

Listen to Nan lead this meditation at nanlundeen.com.

Lie down or sit with your spine straight and your feet flat on the floor. Focus on your breath. Breathe slowly and deeply. Count silently. Breathe in: one—two—three—four. Breathe out: one—two—three—four. Breathe in: one—two—three—four. Breathe out: one—two—three—four. Continue breathing and counting. When thoughts intrude, let them drift by like fluffy clouds on a warm summer day. Continue deep breathing and counting. Relax. Take a deep breath. Allow yourself to finish this sentence: I love to _____. Repeat as often as you like. When you're ready, come back into the here and now.

writing exercises

- Continue daily physical exercise of your choice, Moo stone meditation, and freewriting.

- Take an 8 ½ x 11 piece of paper and fill both sides with the sentences, I love to _____ (fill in the blanks).

- Non-writing exercise: choose one of the things you love to do and do it.

- Paint word pictures. Choose pictures from books or the Internet that pique your imagination. Write descriptions that make the pictures come alive in the mind for someone who hasn't seen the visual art. Example: I found a photo of a Ural owl on the *National Geographic* website. Here's what I wrote: "The white and gray owl floated in space, her wide wings spreading through sky. A heart-shaped helmet of black and white framed her face which was dominated by small black oval eyes. I could feel her focus. A creature of stunning beauty, she intended to kill."

- Play with color. Pick a color you love and a color you hate. Write lines about each, explaining your feelings. Example: "I love turquoise because it carries me back on waves of memory to the Caribbean where my son lives— the sea breeze, the blazing sun, the sense of family holding me like a happy hermit crab tucked into a warm bowl of sand. Although I generally enjoy the color red, I hate red dye in pills. When I must take medicine, I fear the dye will make me sicker than I already am. They lie in my palm and wink at me with ill intent."

- Pick a word that you like. I like the word, "ring." Use it in as many forms as you can conjure up and see if anything stirs your interest. For instance:

  a) "I'd like to hear from you, you master of illusion, so give me a ring on my cell phone."

  b) "Why is that ring on her finger when it should be on mine?"

c) "A ring-tailed squirrel rang our doorbell."

d) "That far-off ringing reminded Grandma of the bell tolling in her village when Geraldine died."

e) "I rang Barry to ask if he knew who stole the statue of Mark Twain from in front of the campus library."

f) "Go ahead and growl at me again, but you need to know you've wrung the last ounce of tears out of my lonely eyes." Oops! Wrong rung. Oh, well, let's just clamber up the ladder of our follies one rung at a time.

- Write nonsense. A poem or a story could emerge. For instance, "The butterfly knew the honey should be saved for the buttercups. They always pouted when they didn't get their share."

- Rearrange words in a sentence or a stanza and see what happens. For instance, I wrote a poem that begins, "I love corn on the cob." What if I changed it to, "Corn on the cob loves me." Or, "The cob wants lots of love but she worries she'll be judged as corny." Silliness oftentimes leads somewhere, although not necessarily where you want to go. The corn progression could transition into a story about a woman who wants to risk loving someone, but struggles with her fear that her expression of love will be judged corny. She begins a search for sophisticated ways to express love, and chaos ensues.

- Page through a dictionary and pick words that appeal to you or pick them at random. Add whatever you need and arrange them into a poem, sentences, or a story. For instance, I just picked "unbolt, opiate, petite, putrid, meet, conquest, bookworm, scrag, and woozy."

- List people and/or animal companion names that appeal to you. Research their meanings. Create a poem or story peopled by characters whose actions reflect their names' meanings. Here's a sample list: Ralph (wolf counsel); Victoria (victory); Jason (healer); Barbara (strange, foreign); David (beloved); Lolita (sorrows).

- Play with onomatopoeia (the use of words that imitate the sound they denote). Here are a few examples: neigh, achoo, hiss, moo, ticktock, quack, zoom, ding, fizz, shush, plunk. "'Achoo!' blew Elsie the cow who had eschewed the moo ever since she learned to hiss. Her friend the duck tried to shush her, offering her a fizzy drink of ding-ding, but she plunked it on the ground and said, 'ticktock, your time of quacking at me to moo is kaput!' 'Neigh,' said the duck."

- Have fun making a list of words to play with starting with a particular letter. Here is one Moo workshop writer's list of favorite "W" words: "wonder, wish, whisper, willow, wind, want, wizard, wheel, wee, wise, wistful." Smash words you like into any order. Here are phrases Moo writers came up with that could spark their imaginations: "cracking spring, willow road river, hungry day feeling." Toss your words together with other words to make a story or a poem.

tips

- When writing a poem, you needn't ask *what does this mean* or worry yourself about how to make it more than it is. Let it be what it is. Therein lies meaning.

- Create pictures with your words. When writing poetry, be aware that sometimes one or several images can make a complete poem. They can be a grace unto themselves.

- Play with point of view. Write a few paragraphs or a stanza from a variety of points of view and see what happens. For instance, try your story in third person omniscient (he, she, they) in which the reader is presented with what's going on in several characters' heads. For example, Tolstoy's *Anna Karenina*. Switch to first person (I) in which one character is the narrator, and the reader sees everything through his or her eyes. Private eye novels often are written first person. Second person (you) sometimes works well in a poem. Maxine Kumin uses the second person powerfully to indict black ops torturers in her poem, "What You Do." Experiment. Study points of view. You'll discover many nuances.

moo notes

moo notes

moo notes

chapter 9
sweet abundance

Belief in an abundance of words is self-fulfilling.

In the comic strip, *Peanuts*, Linus waits every Halloween with sincere faith for the Great Pumpkin to arrive. How you view Linus depends upon what you believe. If you believe the Great Pumpkin will never come, you may ache for him, so naive and innocent. If you believe it is only a matter of time, climb into the pumpkin patch with him. He'll share his blanket with you.

We each are blessed with a Great Pumpkin brimming with words. Choose to have faith like Linus and believe they will be there when you need them.

Reject a self-limiting mindset. It's debilitating. Unlike Linus, some writers believe that an abundance of words waiting to well up from within their subconscious is a myth. They are nervous—may I say selfish—about sharing their words because somebody might steal their ideas. They doubt that if they write a good book a second one would materialize. They measure their creative output in teaspoons, sure that if they write a good poem today, expecting another and another would be foolish. Theirs is a philosophy of self-limitation. These misanthropic writers, standing alongside Linus, wait shriveled like emaciated, defeated scarecrows from whom stuffing is leaking, all the while trying to cover holes in their bodies with scrawny hands inadequate to the task.

How do we become more like Linus?

How about employing a favorite Moo tool—an affirmation. What would make a good writerly abundance affirmation? Remember, we need something short, positive, and in present tense. How about: *I am open to abundance, or imaginative words flow abundantly,* or *I love my imagination?*

Try freewriting a list of affirmations and choose one to stick on your refrigerator.

I'm convinced that a deep pool of creativity lies within each of us. It's a matter of becoming aware.

As abundant as ideas are, they can be fleeting. Have you ever dreamed up a fantastic story idea, were positive you didn't need to write it down, and then wailed later when you discovered you'd forgotten to close the gate and it had wandered off?

Some gifts float by on the stream of consciousness and must be plucked out and put down or they will float on to that great place where all ideas party together and ignore parental orders to come home.

Tune into your inner voice so that you recognize an idea when it surfaces. Listen for a sentence or a phrase. Are characters speaking to you from a piece of fiction in progress? Are nascent characters anxious to escape from your subconscious onto a page?

Creative nubs will float into your life while you're in the shower, during a conversation, or while planting lilies. How about netting them and storing them in an idea box? Decorate a box, choose a jar in a thrift shop, or create an idea folder on your computer. Stuff your ideas in one of those.

Moo workshop writers have fun choosing idea boxes. One woman found a beautifully decorated box on a business trip to Mexico. Another recycled a large wooden box originally used to transport liquor. Another dedicated a dresser drawer. Mine is a wooden recipe box with the word "ideas" stamped on the side and a primitive country scene with red barns and a white house painted on the lid by a friend.

The presence of an idea box in your life will bring comfort even if you never need it. It's backup in case you fear you've run dry.

I recently opened mine and sorted through snips of paper to find two fun titles: "The Terrible Vegetarian" and "The Ladybug Who Preferred to Read." A third is a newspaper clipping, dateline Honolulu, with the headline, "Man allegedly beaten by anger counselor dies." You're free to steal those ideas.

My worst fear when I began creating my own material after years of working as a journalist was dearth of imagination. Would the words be there when I sat down to write my own stuff? If I found all the words for the first project, would words for the second one come along? Do I have anything to say?

I discovered the subconscious is an extraordinary storehouse of imagination and ideas. Not only are the words there, but also their interaction—ways to connect them and create something new. Tap into Moo of

Writing. Hear the words. Hear the stories. Moo is a kind of faith—a faith that the words are there waiting for you.

When you experience an abundant imagination, writing becomes a joy, not a struggle. Words, sentences, paragraphs, chapters, whole books flow. If you're not hearing something you're working on, it may not be the right time for that piece of work to manifest. Turn to some other project. Has the alternative project been clamoring in the back of your mind for attention all along?

I used to believe that if something was really hard, if a task required a huge struggle, if I had to battle to make it happen, it must be worthwhile. I don't believe that anymore. Age has taught me there is a flow and a rhythm to life and what we accomplish. If you work at something, and it makes you miserable, quit. Don't try, try again. Do it differently. Or do something altogether different. Pay attention to the feedback life supplies you. There's a practical reason why "go with the flow" is a cliché. It works!

If you're interested in earning your living as a writer, you must have faith in yourself and a strong belief in word abundance. Know that your imagination is fecund; it holds the seeds of many green, leafy, soul-nutritious words; know that words and ideas and stories lie waiting in us all. Some people choose to write them down.

If you are a Linus, you can be an assistant to the Great Pumpkin of Ideas. Practice. Jot down ideas whether they whisper to you or whack you on the head. There's something about the act of writing that taps abundance. I don't know how that works. I suspect one would have to study linguistics, genetics, mysticism, neuroscience, the collective unconscious, and on and on. Or you can simply choose to accept it as a mysterious process that works.

Listen carefully to your idea box. If it moos, your creative life is fertile. If it snores, nudge yourself and pay closer attention to your inner voice.

Moo.

meditative writing

Listen to Nan lead this meditation at nanlundeen.com.

Choose either an art print or a piece of music that you love. Get into a comfortable position, feet flat on the floor, back straight. Focus on the print or listen to the music, or both. Relax. Breathe deeply several times. Relax. When you feel ready, begin writing words without pausing. Continue freely. Breathe. When you are finished, enjoy the sensation.

A personal note: for meditative writing, I love Georgia O'Keeffe's vibrant flower swirls and the exuberance of Felix Mendelssohn's *A Midsummer Night's Dream*. At other times, Monet's dreamy, ephemeral landscapes and Mozart's optimistic, light-hearted *Concerto for Flute and Harp* inspire me. My husband bangs away on his keyboard with Neil Young tunes blasting. Some good farmers have found that country and western tunes piped into the dairy barn encourage the flow.

writing exercises

- Continue physical exercise of your choice, daily Moo stone meditation, and freewriting.

- Create or find an idea box. Label and decorate it. Use any container that appeals to you such as a jar, a pot, a basket, or a digital folder. When a writing idea or an observation tickles your imagination, write it down and put it in the box.

- Brainstorm paths for your stories to take. Ask, "what if?" as recommended by Anne Bernays and Pamela Painter in their book, *What If? Writing Exercises for Fiction Writers.* If you're not sure where you want your story to go next, jot down at least five ideas. One of them will jump out at you. Do that at any point in your writing just for fun.

tips

- "Threes" satisfy whether you're touting an idea, setting a mood, or weaving a theme in fiction or nonfiction. Introduce it, come around to it again somewhere in the middle, and strike its note again at the end. Threes satisfy the reader's innate sense of abundance. In his short story, "Barn Burning," William Faulkner mentions the smell of cheese in the first line describing the store in which the Justice of the Peace sat. Cheese comes around twice more in that story.

If threes satisfy, will more make us truly happy?

Sometimes. Word repetition can rock with a rhythm of its own. How do you know if repetition works or is boringly redundant? Listen. Always listen as you write. Poetry can benefit from repetition; so can other forms of writing. In "Barn Burning," Faulkner describes the father, who is one of his famous Snopes characters, as wearing a stiff or iron-like black coat at least nine times. The description rhythmically hammers into the reader's mind and imprints an image, leaving a sense of the man's character like indelible ink.

- When listing items whether two, three, or more, list the shortest words first and the items with the longest number of words or syllables last, progressively. The progression aids flow. Example: soda, ice cream, and hazelnuts. Not hazelnuts, soda, and ice cream or some other version. Read the two examples aloud to hear the difference.

- Avoid an abundance of "to be" verbs. When you spot a bunch, ask your Great Pumpkin for a livelier way of saying what you want to express. For instance, "She was a lovely woman" becomes "Loveliness gathered around her like gentle snow."

moo notes

moo notes

chapter 10
which *you* do you trust?

When you write, do you write to please yourself or to please somebody else? Are you staying true to the *you* revealed with the help of your Moo stone?

Go deep and trust your Moo stone self.

People are complicated critters. Our personalities have many aspects. Live the authentic you and walk a path of wisdom.

There's a certain lightness, a kind of fun, a sense of rightness when you're heeding your own compass. Sometimes, wonderful writing happens as if it has a life of its own. It's that quiet voice in the cupboard among your grandmother's tea cups, the ones with the delicate flowers; or it's a nudge just before you're falling asleep; or it's a dream.

Moo workshop participants say they write to inspire, to educate, to create laughter, to make sense of things, or to synthesize experience. Others say, "it puts me in the present," or, "it puts things in perspective," or, "it makes me feel less lonely."

Indeed, connecting with others drives writers. And because society molds us to act as it believes we *should*, we tune in to how others respond to us and trust the counsel of others more than our own.

Do you know writers who are freethinkers? Maybe yourself?

Society exacts conformity, and our own families may hold expectations that are anathema to us. They may mean well. That only makes matters worse. We can sneak about in disguise, but it's more fun to be integrated, to be who you truly are on the outside as well as the inside.

You are the only one who knows what you want to do with your life. If your friends or family think you're wacko, find support elsewhere. If you worry about being selfish, know that when you please yourself, you'll have more joy and love to share.

I'm not suggesting that you quit your day job or that you neglect responsibilities, only that you heed a deep responsibility to yourself.

J.K. Rowling, for example, listened to her deepest self as she wrote her first Harry Potter book, ignoring the convention that suggests children won't read thick, heavy books and that a book can't appeal to people of diverse ages. The commitment to write what you truly love as Rowling did requires stick-to-itiveness.

Employ your Moo stone to help you face fear and self-doubt, those cronies of conventionality. Some part of you may fear that you will crawl blithely out onto a limb of your imagination unaware that some awful specter of reality is slithering up the tree, hacksaw in hand. Simply sitting with those feelings, holding your Moo stone, can decommission them.

That doesn't mean you ought not to spend time questioning your motives. Greed is nasty, for instance, and does not represent our true selves. At times, your path ahead may be mired in the fog of confusion. At such times, let the writing itself be your guide.

I struggled for months to write a poem about a striking secret I learned from a cousin about my paternal grandmother. The words refused to come onto the page. I believed telling the powerful event she chose to keep secret and triumphed over would strengthen the book of poems as memoir I was writing. I finally realized it wasn't mine to tell, and I couldn't ask Grandma's permission because she left this world decades ago. A poem celebrating her strength eventually appeared on the page without revealing all. For a while, I had lost my moral compass, my true and better self, because I was fixed on the prize.

Had I not written the early versions and grappled with the issue, however, the final poem would have been stillborn. We do have shredders and delete buttons, and there's always the bonfire option.

How each writer uses material borrowed from other peoples' lives is a personal decision. Some writers plunder the riches of family dramas to the nth degree and would disagree with my decision about my grandmother. Pat Conroy, who wrote novels inspired by his troubled family, set aside the construct of fiction to write his memoir, *The Death of Santini: The Story of a Father and His Son*. He wrote starkly of abuse. On National Public Radio's "Here & Now" in 2013 he told interviewer Robin Young that he believes his readers expect truth from him and that he tries to provide as much truth as he can get out of himself.

If you're struggling with how much of your personal life to use in your writing, be mindful that material you're uncertain of can fester in your soul and divert your focus, sapping productivity. Drag it out into the light, make a decision, and move on.

At other times, writing flows with lovely energy onto the page, and you seem only to be a conduit.

I was driving back to Marlboro, Massachusetts, where we used to live, from an appointment in New Haven when the outline for this book came to me, every chapter. I later realized the chapter headings would make topics for workshops. I don't advise that people ruminate while driving, however. I missed my exit and became aware of it when I neared downtown Boston forty minutes later.

Stories that want to be told will come through. Relax and let them come. Our world needs stories. They provide oneness, reminding us we are not alone. What grand companions written words are. A storyteller shares his or her take on life at the moment of writing. There may be no intention to share a broad view on the meaning of existence, but the writer can't avoid it, even if his perspective centers on a dearth of meaning.

Who are the writers who bring gifts into your life?

When I was a child, Robert Louis Stevenson's *A Child's Garden of Verses* spoke to me. When I was a teenager, the Russians—Tolstoy and Pasternak—captured my imagination. When, as an adult, I struck out on my own intending to become an independent woman, Marge Piercy's work became a beacon. Later, May Sarton's writing persona became my role model, especially through her journals. Another New England poet, Robert Frost, speaks to my heart. How could I have lived without ever having read "The Road Not Taken?" Maya Angelou's work moves me. I adore Mary Oliver's poetry, and now in my seventies, I appreciate Dickens's delight in the language more than ever. If I had to name a favorite contemporary author, it would be Barbara Kingsolver.

I'm immensely grateful that every one of those writers plumbed the depths of their true selves, and my gratitude goes out to all writers who bare their hearts to share their impressions of this strange and wonderful thing called life.

Lovely, but what about money?

The publishing business is undergoing a sea change with the path forward obscure. There's much you can do in this digital age to market your work and share it with readers. Maybe money will flow your way and maybe not. The best way to attract money is not to set about writing grimly, shoulders tense, determined to make a buck. Such determination is a heavy load for creativity to bear. The best way to attract good money energy is to have fun writing.

magical writing meditation

Listen to Nan lead this meditation at nanlundeen.com.

Seat yourself comfortably with pen at hand. Take several deep breaths. Relax. All is well. Breathe slowly and deeply. Count silently. Breathe in: one—two—three—four. Breathe out: one—two—three—four. Breathe in: one—two—three—four. Breathe out: one—two—three—four. Continue breathing and counting. When thoughts intrude, let them drift by like fluffy clouds on a warm summer day. Now, imagine that you are transported to a fabulously comfortable and beautiful place of your choosing. You are seated in this place. Slowly, look around and take it in. It is your very own favorite place. What do you see? What do you hear? What do you taste and smell? Look down at your lap and find a magical writing tool. You decide to delight yourself in this paradise through your own writing. Let your heart speak to you. In your deepest feelings, what do you want to write?

In real life, pick up your pen now, and begin writing, "I want to write_____."

When you're ready, come back into the here and now.

writing exercises

- Continue daily physical exercise of your choice, Moo stone meditation, and freewriting.

- Write an honest story to yourself about who you are.

tip

- Make your own rules. Wield your powerful pen as you like. We've all been advised, "Show don't tell." Poet Mary Oliver dared to break that rule in her book of poems *American Primitive*, which won the Pulitzer Prize for Poetry. In her poem, "Web," she repeats a line about fear. To see how she makes that work, look up the poem. Reading her work offers rich rewards. This particular line begins with the word, "so." I can imagine some writing instructor somewhere saying, "Mary, first of all, never begin a line with that weak word, 'so.' And secondly, you need to *show* us, not *tell* us, what fear is." Indeed, Oliver does show us, but read the poem without the *telling* line about fear. Are you glad Oliver had the personal sense of power to include it? (Twice!)

moo notes

moo notes

chapter 11
fences

Now that your five gallons of words are flowing every day, what's next? Is it time to share your work? How do you share astutely, protecting yourself and your work?

Build good fences.

Cows need pastures, not confinement in small spaces. They need fences, fences that are sturdy enough to keep out predators, open enough to let in air, and gates that are wise enough to know when to open and when to close.

Fences provide protection.

Do writers need protection?

You bet! You've invested your best energies in your writing. You and your writing deserve to be treated with respect in the marketplace. Vet the places you will submit your work whether for representation or publication. Take risks, but do so wisely.

Before you open the gate, create the strongest work possible. When it's ready, give it to someone you trust to read. For early feedback some writers rely on a first reader, and some rely on a group of peers.

Have you chosen your first reader judiciously?

One Moo workshop writer said the first person she would show her manuscript to "definitely" would be her husband. She should suit up in mental armor, not that her husband would intentionally hurt her. But asking for first-reader feedback from someone she's close to gives his criticism a lot of power. It would be easy to take her husband's comments straight to heart regardless of their accuracy. That doesn't mean it can't work. If she's lucky, he may be the perfect first reader. She needs to give her decision some thought.

I am enormously grateful to my husband for his feedback and editing. We're both wordsmiths; we share a background in journalism. Writers who can depend on their first reader to be honest and kind are blessed. Not all partners or first readers, however, know how to critique without wounding. It's a skill. Negative criticisms, even those stemming from the best of intentions, are the most difficult to detach from when offered by folks who mean the most to us. Overly charitable feedback given because our people love us can be nearly as damaging.

Still, you'll notice that many authors thank their spouse, a relative, or a close friend in their published works. A relationship involving manuscript feedback can be workable and imminently useful. You can nurture the writer-reader relationship even with someone close to you and remain centered and detached.

Critique groups in person or online can be valuable beyond measure. Search for colleagues who will be honest, who will say what does and what doesn't work for them, and who make suggestions, all delivered in the spirit of helpful criticism.

Return the favor.

Marge Piercy says in *So You Want to Write*, a book she co-authored with Ira Wood, that it's vital to be mindful of what your workshop colleagues want to write, not what you think they should write. I would add—or the style you think they should write it in. I've seen fledgling critique group participants lose inspiration and become disillusioned because their style was wordier than the group felt was appropriate. And this on a first draft! I've dabbled in magical realism, and that often throws a group into a tizzy, but not always.

Listen with an open mind to a critique of your work and consider its merits. You needn't embrace every criticism, agonize over it, and reconsider whether you have any future whatsoever as a writer.

In my workshops, I ask whether participants feel that writers by the nature of their vocation make themselves vulnerable. After all, we're sharing our treasured imaginative work that comes from within. Moo workshop writer Cathy Zellmann says she prefers the word "open" to "vulnerable." To her, "vulnerable" connotes "victim."

And victims we are not.

How do you know when you attend a new critique group whether the butterflies in your stomach are fluttering a valid warning or simply signifying discomfort in a new and risky situation?

Does the feeling keep coming around? You could set a number of times you will attend and reserve judgment until you've put in your time. If the negative feeling clamors for attention, chuck the group and move on. Search for critique groups online, at bookstores, libraries, and in writers' organizations. If you don't find one you're comfortable with, start one.

When you find a group you like, detach from critiques and decide for yourself what you want to rewrite and what you don't. If you disagree with an assessment, you can, of course, choose to ignore it rather than be wounded by it. What if the group irritates you, or all you hear is pabulum such as, "I like this," spoken as if they were sincere? Does anyone produce a perfect manuscript? Search for a more useful group.

At times, you will hear criticisms that you don't want to hear. Keep in mind that the criticism may be valid even if offered in a blunt way. Think it through as objectively as you can.

On the other hand, some writers are mean, just as some people in general are. Who knows what their motives are? Maybe they're insecure, ignorant, misguided, narcissistic, egotistical, or just plain jealous. If the rest of the group is beneficial, decide whether you want to put up with the aggravation. Another option would be to stand up to the bully assertively but not aggressively at every opportunity. You have to be tough to accomplish that. Are you? It's more difficult if you're the only person the bully picks on. If someone keeps lobbing mean critiques at you, does the group's culture encourage that behavior? If you love the group except for one or two problematic people that you feel attack you personally, it's good to remember the problem lies with them, not with you or your work.

I attended a critique group where a man accused a poet, I will call Ann, of using big words as a means of showing off her vocabulary. To the contrary, Ann delights in playing with words, and years later, she still revisits his insult with anger.

If you were Ann, could you have ignored the critique? It's more important than any of us realize to wield the red pen lightly. Personal attacks can wound others. The man who was discombobulated by big words could have said the poem contained several words he was unfamiliar with, making the meaning unclear to him. The poet could choose to simplify or not.

When offering criticism, no matter the topic, begin with the word, "I," not the word, "you." So, avoid saying, "You have written an unclear sentence." Instead say, "I don't quite get this sentence. It's unclear to me."

Give at least two positive comments for every comment that could be construed as negative. Above all, writers need encouragement.

North Carolina poet Diana Pinckney, told her audience at a poetry workshop in Rock Hill, South Carolina, in June 2012 that she relies on feedback from two critique groups. The poet, who won the 2012 Grand Prize in the *Atlanta Review*'s International Poetry Competition, said she listens and decides what is useful. The rest she lets "roll like water off a duck's back."

How do you know what's useful?

If something sticks with you, pay attention to it, Pinckney said. The mean guy's criticism sure stuck with Ann, the problem being she made a decision to continue delighting in words of her choosing, but didn't do the duck bit and let go after she decided.

I pay attention when I hear the same criticisms coming from more than one reader. For instance, when I was writing this manuscript, I used language such as, "may" and "would" and "could" as in "you may try this or that."

The reason?

I hate bossy how-to-write manuals. Two readers said I sounded wishy-washy as if unsure of my advice. "Be more assertive," one reader said. She even advised using an exclamation point now and then!

Did I follow the advice?

I aimed for middle ground between bossiness that would raise peoples' hackles and namby-pamby drivel. Did I succeed? Visit me at nanlundeen. com to send me a message and let me know.

Don't focus on negative criticism and ignore positive feedback. I don't know why we hang onto negative criticism as if we're clutching a chunk of floating wood in the middle of the Pacific. Write compliments down and display them in your writing nook. The rest of the time, imitate a duck.

When do you take a manuscript to a critique group?

Some writers share a first draft, and others like to polish their work before they risk reading it to anyone, even the barn cat. First-draft advocates want to know if their vision is manifesting as they intend in the eyes of readers before they invest too much time. Those who edit and rewrite before sharing are wary of falling into a muddle from too many suggestions during a first draft. They want to hearken to their own muse.

When you have critiques in hand, give yourself ample time to mull over potential changes. Befriend time. Works in progress benefit from rest. Time gives writers an extremely valuable gift—perspective. Let feedback percolate at least overnight. Don't leave it too long, or you'll forget the nuances of what people said. I sometimes take my laptop with me and jot notes in the manuscript as people critique, let it sit overnight, and tackle it the next day. My decision to change or not to change often appears at dawn.

Are you considering paying a consulting editor to critique your work? Many writers' conferences offer one-on-one critiques for a price, and they abound online.

If you decide to do this, check your fences.

No matter how highfalutin the credentials are, consultants can't help you unless they're caring people. Become a part of the literary community where you live and watch out for each other. Find at least two people who've had critiques by this consultant and ask if the critiques were helpful, how and why. If you consult a professional, stay centered and detached just as you would with your critique group.

Several years ago, I paid a consultant to critique the first thirty-five pages and synopsis of a mystery novel I was writing. He eviscerated the plot. My manuscript retreated into a closet and stayed there. Because I lacked self-confidence, I gave that man an inappropriate amount of power. Recently, I pulled it out and looked at it again. It's actually quite strong. Even if it were as flawed as he said, why be brutal?

When a friend confronted him about his brutish behavior, he said, "I thought that was what she wanted."

Rapists say the same thing.

Before you can draw on fierceness and tenacity to stand up for your work, it must be the best it can be. Your fences will hold firm only if you are self-confident. Edit draft after draft with a hard pen. Be tough on yourself. Pare, whittle, question. Give yourself good reason to believe in your work. Deal from strength. You will need it to parry the slings and arrows of the marketplace. And keep in mind many supportive, appreciative readers are waiting for your words.

Editing and rewriting can be daunting tasks because they feel as if they go on forever. Do you have trouble imagining eternity? Chances are you haven't edited and rewritten a book-length manuscript, edited again and rewritten again and on and on. I do recall, however, that in chapter 7, I wrote, "Adopting a positive attitude is the most important thing you will ever do." I confess I'm not taking my own advice and staying positive about rewriting. I'm working on that. Whether writing poetry, fiction, or nonfiction, I'll look for the joy in shaping the manuscript to become better and stronger. To make the task less onerous, my goal will be to relax and enjoy playing with the language to make it as lively as possible.

What if your creative Child wants to write something new when you're already enveloped by a project you want to finish?

Bargain with your Kid and balance time between creating new stuff and bringing projects to fruition, including spending time marketing. If you close the Kid out, he'll rebel, creating havoc with your writing life. Consult your Moo stone and make decisions accordingly. Do what works best for you.

When is a work finished?

There may always be a niggling sense of doubt about a manuscript. If it's stronger than niggling, take another look. If you're not sure, consult your gut. Mend your fences; be sure your manuscript is squeaky clean.

Reading your work aloud catches errors, irregular rhythm, and repetitiveness. Listen as if you were a parent attuned to your child napping in the next room. Also, reading a printout will catch mistakes long after you believe your manuscript is pristine. Letting it rest gives you a fresh eye. Use spell-check only as a supplement. Don't rely on it. It won't catch homophones such as "hair" and "hare," or "there" and "their," for instance.

Eat with, sleep with, and reread often Strunk and White's *The Elements of Style*.

Double-check the spelling of names when writing nonfiction. People use the most imaginative spellings for names including those that sound traditional.

In fiction, check for internal consistency. As you write, keep cheat sheets listing your characters and their characteristics so that Jane doesn't have blond hair in one chapter and brown in another. Create a timeline so that you'll know whether a character was born after an historic event he attended, or if you birthed a child in the wrong decade, or if Jan mentions Carl's irritating habit of slurping his coffee before she's met him. Historical novelists research without ceasing. If you're writing fantasy or an alternate universe, keep track of details about the world you're creating; this is especially helpful when writing a series. Cheat sheets will save you gobs of editing time.

After you've listened to feedback, after you've edited and rewritten, it's time to open the gate to the outside world. Publication takes us back to the question asked in chapter 6: why do you write? Know your purpose and your market before you choose a publication path.

One of my friends is putting together a memoir of vignettes for her grandchildren about growing up in a military family. She's considering printing them as spiral-bound books at an office supply store. Another is creating a cookbook from her North Carolina mountain heritage; she'll include her photography and anecdotes about the women whose recipes she shares. She's considering print on demand, a service offered by publishers that prints books from a digital platform as they are ordered.

To make it happen, envision your finished work at any point in the Moo process. Quickly without thinking much, pick up a pencil and sketch your title, your byline, and a brief indication of how you want your work to materialize.

When Moo workshop writer Angie Feltman heard this suggestion, she thought she had nothing to draw, but she picked up a pencil and put it to paper, anyway.

"There it is," she said. "Of course."

Here's a caveat—the Moo process can dry up on a get-rich-quick mentality. There's something about a my-creativity-must-make-money attitude that shrivels the creative process. I must share with you, though, that I heard a best-selling author give a speech at a writers' conference saying that he had set out to write a blockbuster, and that's exactly what he achieved. For other best-selling authors, luck is a huge factor. All of them have one thing in common, however. They sit down and actually write. As we discussed in chapter 10, the best path to attracting money is having fun writing. Play. Enjoy the process.

Don't let the sun go down upon your rejections. Send the manuscript out the same day a rejection comes in. When possible, send your work to places that accept multiple submissions. Be sure to let them know immediately when your work is accepted elsewhere. The question often arises whether it's okay to submit to more than one publishing venue if they don't accept multiple submissions. That's an ethical question to be decided by the individual. Are you willing to risk irritating a publisher who invests time in considering your work and you pull it? Ask yourself how much time you want to invest waiting for responses. Some publishers respond in three months or longer. Do you have that kind of time to submit your work exclusively?

If you choose the traditional publication route, expect your agent and editors to ask for rewrites. Don't overreact. Adopt a professional attitude. Be courteous, businesslike, and cooperative, but if your gut rebels on this or that point, stand up for your writing. An effective fence stands firm during the harshest of winter storms.

Many writers enjoy success with reputable independent publishers. The good indies provide competent editing, personal attention, and marketing help.

Michel Stone found success with an independent publisher. Her novel, *The Iguana Tree*, published by Spartanburg, South Carolina-based Hub City Press, won a bronze medal for literary fiction in the 2012 Independent Publisher Book Awards. Hub City, which publishes four or five books a year, gives "every book they publish lots of attention," Stone said. "My publisher also serves as my publicist. She and I work together to get my novel exposure. Hub City makes me feel like my book's success is as important to the press as it is to me."

Given the digital revolution in publishing, new pathways present a sweet abundance of ways to share your work. Research the pros and cons of each. Look at self-publishing, print on demand, and ebooks. The stigma of self-publishing is vanishing and will disappear in two shakes of a cow's tail as more self-published writers frolic in a meadow green with money.

If you decide to self-publish, editing becomes even more important. Do everything in your power to make your manuscript error free. If you're uncomfortable with your editing skills, educate yourself or hire a professional.

Decide early on whether you want to quote published material. If so, set about getting permissions from the copyright owners. Copyright law allows exceptions for fair use; unfortunately, the law is muddy, and findings on whether or not you infringed on copyright may be decided by a court if you run afoul of the copyright owner or are perceived as having done something wrong. Even one line can cause grief. Discovering who owns the copyright can be downright perplexing, as can determining whether the material is in the public domain. And those are only the first steps. Permissions take time, can cost money, and can involve legal fees. Attributing the quote doesn't absolve you from blame if you don't have permission to use it. Don't depend on ignorance to protect you.

For an excellent overview of your rights and responsibilities as an author, I highly recommend the book, *The Writer's Legal Guide: An Authors Guild Desk Reference*, by Kay Murray and Tad Crawford.

In general, have fun exploring, but let the Adult part of your personality take over and treat publication as a business. Protect yourself. Be a savvy business person.

Consult an accountant on how to handle your writing finances. You'll be happy you did at tax time.

If you want to find an agent, vet them and find a good one.

Thoroughly research publication choices. When searching for advice on the Internet, pay attention to the URL (Internet address). Look at both the URL and the source's credentials. Rely only on authoritative sources. Use common sense and take nothing at face value. If it doesn't look right, search further. And remember the publishing landscape changes second-by-second. Whoosh! Be nimble! Writers are surfing the waves of future shock.

Nowadays, authors promote their work through blogs, tweets, websites, and all sorts of social media even before it's published. Harness your creativity to market your work whether you take a traditional or more innovative path to publication. Say hello to the little red hen. Remember the folk tale? The little red hen couldn't get anybody to help with the work, so she did it herself. And reaped the benefits.

Productive dairy cows and marketing-marvel red hens have been happily co-existing for years. The best marketing tool is new, high quality material—more and more and more buckets brimming with milk.

detachment meditation

Listen to Nan lead this meditation at nanlundeen.com.

Print the title page of your manuscript. Sit with it in your lap, holding it with both hands. Breathe deeply and relax. Count silently. Breathe in: one—two—three—four. Breathe out: one—two—three—four. Breathe in: one—two—three—four. Breathe out: one—two—three—four. Continue breathing and counting. When thoughts intrude, let them drift by like fluffy clouds on a warm summer day. Now, feel a summer breeze touching your face. How does it smell? Feel the breeze tickling your nose and cooling your body. Take a deep breath. Relax. Enjoy the breeze. Enjoy the sun on your face. Sit quietly and breathe. Now, open your hands and give your page to the breeze. Let go. When you feel ready, come back into the here and now. Peace.

writing exercises

- Continue daily physical exercise of your choice, Moo stone meditation, and freewriting.

- With a good, up-to-date dictionary and *The Chicago Manual of Style* at your elbow, line-edit a piece of your writing for spelling, punctuation, grammar, and flow. Run spell-check to catch spelling errors, but don't rely on it. Consult *The Associated Press Stylebook* if you're writing for news organizations. *The Elements of Style* by William Strunk, Jr. and E.B. White is vital to your writing life.

tips

- Be alert to goop words—commonly misspelled, misused words that can goop up your writing. Begin your own file of them and invest in a good word book such as *Woe Is I: The Grammarphobe's Guide to Better English in Plain English* by Patricia T. O'Conner. Here's a sample list of goop words:

affect – effect
its – it's
well – good
accept – except
alternate – alternative
among – between
choose – chose
loose – lose
compliment – complement
imply – infer
farther - further
sit - set
fewer – less than
irregardless – regardless
lay – laid – had laid
lie – lay – had lain
principal – principle
flounder - founder
stationary – stationery

Word usage changes, so keep an up-to-date usage dictionary on your favorites list or at hand. For instance, "well" and "good" have progressed to a state of flux as in, "How are you today? Good, thanks."

How do you feel about the proclivity some folks have to use "like" as a substitute for the word, "said?" ("And I'm like, 'I don't want to see that stupid movie,' and he's like, 'sure you do.'")

- Editing tips:
  - » Keep cheat sheets to track details. There's software available for that.
  - » Check for internal consistency.
  - » Print your work.
  - » Read aloud to yourself.
  - » Use a minimum of "ing" words.
  - » Use strong verbs.
  - » Use adverbs sparingly.
  - » Use passive voice sparingly.
  - » Be sensitive to pace and flow.
  - » Let it sit.
  - » Workshop it.
  - » Detach and coolly decide which criticisms to accept and which to reject.
  - » Play positive feedback reruns in your head.

- What to cut:

  » Redundancies.

  » Unnecessary words. Pay attention to articles. For instance in the sentence, "I love to lie in the straw under dust motes floating in sunbeams through fly-speckled windows," do you see an unnecessary article?

  » Clichés.

  » Repeated words. Read your work aloud to catch overuse of words within a paragraph or two. There's software that will do that for you, but the ear does a better job.

  » Run-on sentences.

- When you edit, give yourself the "swan test" recommended in chapter 6. See the scene the reader sees evoked by the page, not the scene in your head. The reader has no direct access to your brain, at least not in this decade of the twenty-first century.

- Back up your work. Keep one version off-site.

- If you publish in the United States, register the copyright of your work with the U.S. Copyright Office at copyright. gov. Registration is voluntary but is required if you want to sue for infringement of a U.S. work. Whether you register your work or not, use the copyright symbol, date, and name. For example, ©2014 Jane Doe.

conclusion

Put down this handbook only temporarily. It's your best friend. Return to it to reinforce your Moo practice; ruminate and add notes. Moodle. Listen to the meditations at nanlundeen.com. Encourage the flow by re-doing the exercises that appeal to you. Go for a walk. Let your mind wander. Unmask your fears. Visit your safe space and invite your inner Child to play. Trust yourself. Scratch time behind the ear. Create your own habit loop and skip through it happily day after day like a child skipping rope. Hold your Moo stone in your hand even on your busiest of days lest you forget who you are. Follow your belly wisdom, knowing that at your center lies power. Join Linus in the Great Pumpkin Patch of words for surely a sweet abundance awaits, pooling in anticipation for the pen that belongs to the true Moo of you.

"Moo of Writing works," says freelance writer Mary Ellen Lives. "I just have to remember to do it."

moo notes

moo notes

the moo writer's bookshelf

Angelou, Maya, *Wouldn't Take Nothing for My Journey Now*, (Random House Publishing Group, New York, 1994).

Atwood, Margaret, *Negotiating with the Dead: A Writer on Writing*, (Knopf Doubleday Publishing Group, New York, 2003).

Dillard, Annie, *The Writing Life*, (HarperCollins Publishers, New York, 1990).

Gawain, Shakti, *Developing Intuition: Practical Guidance for Daily Life*, (New World Library, Novato, CA, 2001).

Goldberg, Natalie, *Writing Down the Bones: Freeing the Writer Within*, 2d ed. (Shambhala Publications, Inc., Boston, 2005).

King, Stephen, *On Writing: A Memoir of the Craft*, 10th ann. ed. (Scribner, New York, 2010).

Kipfer, Barbara Ann, *Roget's International Thesaurus*, 7th ed. (HarperCollins Publishers, New York, 2011).

Lamott, Anne, *Bird by Bird: Some Instructions on Writing and Life*, (Knopf Doubleday Publishing Group, New York, 1995).

Merriam-Webster's Collegiate Dictionary, 11th ed. rev. (Merriam-Webster, Inc., Springfield, MA 2003).

Merriam-Webster's Dictionary of English Usage, 2d ed. rev. (Merriam-Webster, Inc., Springfield, MA, 1994).

Murray, Kay and Tad Crawford, *The Writer's Legal Guide: An Authors Guild Desk Reference*, 4th ed. (Allworth Press, Skyhorse Publishing, Inc., New York, 2013).

Myss, Caroline, Ph.D., *Anatomy of the Spirit: The Seven Stages of Power and Healing*, (Crown Publishing Group, New York, 1997).

O'Conner, Patricia T., *Woe Is I: The Grammarphobe's Guide to Better English in Plain English*, (G.P. Putnam's Sons, New York, 1996).

Oliver, Mary, *A Poetry Handbook: A Prose Guide to Understanding and Writing Poetry*, (Houghton Mifflin Harcourt Publishing Company, New York, 1994).

Oliver, Mary, *Rules for the Dance: A Handbook for Writing and Reading Metrical Verse*, (Houghton Mifflin Harcourt Publishing Company, New York, 1998).

Paz, Octavio, *The Other Voice: Essays on Modern Poetry* (Harcourt Brace Jovanovich, Inc., Orlando, FL, 1990).

Piercy, Marge and Ira Wood, *So You Want to Write: How to Master the Craft of Writing Fiction and the Personal Narrative*, (Leapfrog Press, Wellfleet, MA, 2001).

Strunk, William Jr. and E.B. White, *The Elements of Style*, 4th ed. (Longman, London, 1999).

Tan, Amy, *The Opposite of Fate: Memories of a Writing Life*, (Penguin Group USA, Inc., New York, 2004)

Associated Press Stylebook most recent print ed. or *AP Stylebook* online at www.ap.org.

The Chicago Manual of Style the most recent print ed. or online at www.chicagomanualofstyle.org.

Thich Nhat Hanh, *Be Free Where You Are*, (Parallax Press, Berkeley, CA, updated 2013).

Ueland, Brenda, *If You Want to Write*, (first published, 1938, various editions are available).

Walker, Alice, *We Are the Ones We Have Been Waiting For: Inner Light in a Time of Darkness*, (The New Press, New York, 2006).

www.alanrinzler.com/blog

www.publisherslunch.com

www.publishersweekly.com

notes

Chapter 1

http://buddhism.about.com/od/chanandzenbuddhism/a/What-Is-Mu.htm.

Oppezzo, Marily and Daniel L. Schwartz, "Give Your Ideas Some Legs: The Positive Effect of Walking on Creative Thinking," *Journal of Experimental Psychology: Learning, Memory and Cognition*, http://dx.doi.org/10.1037/a0036577, (4-21-2014).

Wong, May, "Stanford study finds walking improves creativity," *Stanford Report*, http://news.stanford.edu/news/2014/april/walking-vs-sitting-042414.html, (4-24-2014).

Walker, Alice, *We Are the Ones We Have Been Waiting For: Inner Light in a Time of Darkness*, (The New Press, New York, 2006).

Ueland, Brenda, *If You Want to Write*, 2d ed. (The Schubert Club, St. Paul, MN, 1984).

Ueland, Brenda, *Me*, (The Schubert Club, St. Paul, MN, 1983).

Bradbury, Ray, *Zen in the Art of Writing: Essays on Creativity*, (Capra Press, Santa Barbara, CA, 1989).

Center for Investigating Healthy Minds at the Waisman Center, University of Wisconsin, Madison. Center founder is Richard J. Davidson, Ph.D. www.investigatinghealthyminds.org.

Goleman, Daniel, Paul Kaufman, and Michael Ray, *The Creative Spirit*, (Dutton, the Penguin Group, New York, 1992).

www.gold.ac.uk/psychology/staff/bhattacharya.

Highfield, Roger, "Relax the brain for that Eureka! moment," http://www.telegraph.co.uk/news/science/science-news/3322773/Relax-the-brain-for-that-Eureka-moment.html, (1-23-2008).

Beilock, Sian, Ph.D., "Want To Be Creative? Let Your Mind Wander," https://www.psychologytoday.com/blog/choke/201210/want-be-creative-let-your-mind-wander, (10-10-2012).

Kaplan, Matt, "Why great ideas come when you aren't trying," http://www.nature.com/news/why-great-ideas-come-when-you-aren-t-trying-1.10678, (5-21-2012).

Tierney, John, "Discovering the Virtues of a Wandering Mind," http://www.nytimes.com/2010/06/29/science/29tier.html?_r=0, (6-28-2010).

Strickler, Jeff, "No lotus position needed: Neuroscience pushes meditation into the mainstream," http://www.startribune.com/lifestyle/health/209378341.html, (5-29-2013).

Chapter 2

Duhigg, Charles, "How Companies Learn Your Secrets," *The New York Times Sunday Magazine*, page MM30, (2-19-2012).

Chapter 3

Harris, Thomas A., M.D., *I'm OK—You're OK*, (HarpersCollins Publishers, New York, 2004.)

Chapter 4

Higginson, William J. and Penny Harter, *The Haiku Handbook: How to Write, Teach, and Appreciate Haiku* (Kodansha USA, Inc., New York, 1985).

Haiku Society of America, Inc. at hsa-haiku.org.

Hay, Louise L., *You Can Heal Your Life*, (Hay House, Inc., Carlsbad, CA, 1984).

Chapter 5

Myss, Caroline, Ph.D., *Anatomy of the Spirit: The Seven Stages of Power and Healing*, (Harmony, New York, 1997).

Gawain, Shakti, *Developing Intuition: Practical Guidance for Daily Life* (New World Library, Novato, CA, 2002).

Chapter 6

Thich Nhat Hanh, *Anger: Wisdom for Cooling the Flames*, (Riverhead Books, New York, 2001).

John 14:27. New International Version.

Chapter 7

Eccl. 3:1. NIV.

Strunk, William Jr. and E.B. White, *The Elements of Style*, 4th ed. (Longman, London, 1999).

Chapter 8

Rhodes, J. Stephen, *The Time I Didn't Know What to Do Next*, (Wind Publications, Nicholasville, KY, 2008).

Kumin, Maxine, *Where I Live: New & Selected Poems 1990-2010*, (W.W. Norton & Company, Inc., New York, 2010).

Chapter 9

Bernays, Anne, and Pamela Painter, *What If? Writing Exercises for Fiction Writers*, (HarpersCollins Publishers, New York, 1991).

Chapter 10

Oliver, Mary, *American Primitive*, (Little, Brown and Company, Boston, 1983).

Young, Robin, "Pat Conroy No Longer Hides Behind Fiction to Tell His Family's Stories," WBUR, National Public Radio, "Here & Now," http://hereandnow.wbur.org/2013/11/19/pat-conroy-santini.

Chapter 11

Piercy, Marge and Ira Wood, *So You Want to Write: How to Master the Craft of Writing Fiction and the Personal Narrative*, (Leapfrog Press, Wellfleet, MA, 2001).

about the author

Photo by Ron DeKett

An award-winning journalist, Nan Lundeen's article, "Find Your Moos," appeared in the U.K.'s *Writing Magazine*. Her columns on writing have appeared in the South Carolina Writers Workshop's *Quill* and at *femalefirst.co.uk*. She has authored two books of poetry, and her work appears in small literary magazines. She holds a bachelor's in English and a master's in communications from Western Michigan University. Contact her through her website at www.nanlundeen.com where you also can arrange for Moo of Writing workshops. She welcomes your comments.

Made in the USA
Monee, IL
05 June 2021